In Search of PHYSICIAN Leadership

Barbara LeTourneau
Wesley Curry

Health Administration Press
Chicago, Illinois

In
Search
of
PHYSICIAN
Leadership

02   01   00   99   98   5   4   3   2   1

Library of Congress Cataloging-in-Publication Data

In search of physician leadership / edited by Barbara LeTourneau and Wesley Curry.
    p.   cm.
    Includes bibliographical references and index.
    ISBN 1-56793-082-4
    1. Physician executives—Vocational guidance.   2. Health services administration.   3. Leadership.   4. Executive ability.
    I. LeTourneau, Barbara.   II. Curry, Wesley.
    [DNLM: 1. Physician Executives.   2. Delivery of Health Care—organization & administration.   W 21 I347 1998]
    RA971.I47   1998
    362.1'068'4—dc21
    DNLM/DLC
    for Library of Congress   98-13927
                              CIP

Health Administration Press
A division of the Foundation
  of the American College of
  Healthcare Executives
One North Franklin Street, Suite 1700
Chicago, IL 60606-3491
312/424-2800

CONTENTS

Introduction

Barbara LeTourneau and Wesley Curry

N O PROFESSION, we think, has been more buffeted by recent trends and events in the healthcare delivery and financing system in the United States than medicine. Once the decision-making captains, both clinically and administratively, of the healthcare ship, physicians have seen their authority and influence slip over the past decades. It should be no surprise, then, that physicians are showing an increasing interest in regaining some of the control they have lost, especially to nonphysicians. The overall thesis of this book is that physicians are entering the management ranks in increasing numbers and in increasingly advanced levels of responsibility and authority. Further, it is the book's contention that this trend portends well for both the medical profession and for the healthcare system that it serves.

The current healthcare system is vastly different than the one physicians dominated earlier in this century. The healthcare product has always been the patient-physician relationship, and prior to 1970, this relationship was very personal and specific to one physician for each patient. Physicians were like artisans—they were experts on medicine and on what would work for individual patients. This cottage industry resulted in many small "shops" geared to the needs of individuals. Most care was provided outside hospitals by private practitioners, who managed

Note: This chapter is based on an article by the authors that appeared in *Frontiers of Health Services Management*, Volume 13, No. 3, published by Health Administration Press.

their own practices, and hospitals were largely owned or operated by physicians. Even when physicians had no financial stake in a hospital, they exercised substantial control either directly, through their involvement in the provision of healthcare services, or indirectly, through their presence on or influence over the board of trustees. Whatever the administration of the hospital, its expenses were dictated by the physicians on its medical staff. Their orders, largely unchallenged, directed financial traffic.

The nonphysician managers of hospitals understood the complexity of the institutions they ran and knew that changes were in order. This was before the passage of the Hill-Burton Act in 1935, but there were already about 5,000 hospitals, and they had become very complex organizations (Neuhauser 1983). Surgery and asepsis had changed both the delivery of medicine and the institutions in which it was delivered. Clinicians would continue to be powerful forces in the delivery of care, but, especially with the formation in 1934 of the American College of Hospital Administrators, now the American College of Healthcare Executives (ACHE), professional managers were now in charge (Neuhauser 1983). Superintendents had become administrators, and would later become presidents in the shift to corporate structures in the 1970s. Only a few very large institutions—usually those that were academic in nature, were still owned by physicians, or were located in the largest of our cities— remained in physician manager hands. In 1985, about 230 of the 6,872 U.S. hospitals had physician administrators or CEOs (*AHA Guide to the Health Care Field, 1986* 1986). There are now closer to 6,300 U.S. hospitals, and the number of physician CEOs has not changed very much, remaining at about 200 (*AHA Guide to the Health Care Field, 1996* 1997).

While the number of physicians in charge of hospitals remains low, the overall number of physicians in management has grown substantially. The membership of the American College of Physician Executives (ACPE) is instructive (see Table 1.1). From the 64 charter members in 1975, when the College was named the American Academy of Medical Directors, membership has grown to more than 12,000 (ACPE 1997). Earlier, the membership was dominated by physicians in group practice and hospital settings. Now, although the largest segments are still in groups, hospitals, managed care organizations, and academic health centers, physician executives are found throughout the healthcare delivery system (see Table 1.2). As indicated in Table 1.3, statistics from the American Medical Association confirm this pattern of growth (*Physician Characteristics and Distribution in the U.S.* 1997).

Although physicians have not risen in substantial numbers to the top of the executive hierarchy, they are occupying an increasing number of middle medical management slots. One suspects that healthcare organi-

Table 1.1 Growth in Membership of the American College of Physician Executives

Year	Membership
1975	64
1976	99
1977	138
1978	188
1979	276
1980	428
1981	616
1982	836
1983	1,085
1984	1,411
1985	1,747
1986	2,244
1987	3,183
1988	4,259
1989	4,898
1990	5,711
1991	6,388
1992	7,174
1993	8,357
1994	9,524
1995	10,909
1996	12,251
1997	12,806

Source: American College of Physician Executives Membership Database

zations have learned what other complicated organizations learned long ago: Provided with proper management training, technical professionals are an excellent source for filling the middle management positions tied most directly to their profession. Engineers are found throughout industry in departments of engineering. Lawyers head legal operations in those firms. It is not that others cannot manage these operations equally well, it is that professionals can combine management skills and familiarity with the technical profession in a way that nonprofessionals simply cannot.

Managing the organization itself is an entirely different matter. It is no secret that many nonphysician healthcare managers view physicians with some alarm and see them as a threat. Even though the number of physician CEOs in healthcare is small—and static—the sheer number of physicians and their growing interest in roles in the management of the healthcare system has made nonphysician managers apprehensive. In

Table 1.2   Organizational Settings of Physician Executives

Hospitals	27.8%
Group Practices	24.8
Managed Care	9.4
Health Systems	4.1
Military	3.0
Consulting	3.6
Ambulatory Care Centers	3.1
Government	2.5
Insurance	3.0
Physician-Hospital Organizations	1.2
Industry	1.4
Contract Management Organizations	0.9
Academic Health Centers	5.9
Other	9.3

Source: American College of Physician Executives Membership Database

Table 1.3   Physicians in Administration

Year	Number
1970	12,158
1975	11,161
1980	12,209
1985	13,810
1990	14,819
1993	14,524
1994	15,684
1995	16,345

Source: Physician Characteristics and Distribution in the U.S. 1997

a healthcare system under siege, the competition for positions is keen, especially at the top. The fears, however, are unrealistic. Physicians have made and will continue to make significant contributions to the management of healthcare organizations. And some of them will continue to rise to top leadership. But they will do so only if they acquire the same high level of demonstrable management expertise that their nonphysician colleagues have had to demonstrate for their management success. And if they *do* acquire the requisite expertise, health organizations would be foolish not to advance them.

What is causing the increased movement of physicians into the management ranks? We would like to dispense with one reason immediately.

It is no secret that growing numbers of physicians are disgruntled. The loss of autonomy and influence upsets them. The loss of income frightens and angers them. The medical literature has become replete with stories of physicians who have left the practice of medicine entirely, sometimes at an earlier than normal retirement age (Starr 1982; Nash 1993; Kushner 1995). Surprising numbers would not repeat their career choices and would not encourage others, particularly their children, to do so. Many of these physicians explore management as an alternative. But if their unhappiness is the primary motivating factor, their failure is probably ensured. And if they believe that management is an easy waystation on the way to retirement and that the skills necessary for success are simple and easily obtained, their failure is guaranteed. A management career in these shifting and dynamic times is not for amateurs or the faint of heart. It is often stated by physician executives that their most difficult tasks are convincing physician colleagues that they are still physicians and nonphysician management colleagues that they deserve to be viewed seriously as managers. An absence of requisite management skills will only increase the skepticism of both sets of colleagues.

We believe that two structural changes in the delivery and financing of healthcare services—managed care and systems integration—are the main impetus for physicians seriously seeking management careers.

The Pressures of Managed Care

Managed care organizations are a long-time factor in the healthcare delivery system beginning with the Ross-Loos Clinics in Southern California in the late 1920s. Recently joined by new managed care entities—preferred provider organizations, independent practice associations, exclusive provider organizations, prepaid group practices, and others—HMOs and their newer iterations are having a substantial impact on the delivery and financing of healthcare services. It could be said that these facilities and delivery systems are essentially "managed cost" organizations. We believe that the pressures for cost containment and reduction—already altering the once freewheeling practice of medicine—would likely have gained momentum even in the absence of the managed care response. Spiraling costs and festering social issues would have eventually forced change. While the approach is primarily through financing methods, the effect is to change practice styles and methods. Physicians are being told by a growing number of nonphysician—and nonclinician—sources how, when, and where to practice medicine.

Is that bad? It depends on the perspective from which one looks. One can hardly fault physicians for wanting far more meaningful input into those decisions. Clearly, physicians desire a voice in the decisions on the rules under which managed care will operate. They also want a voice in how those decisions are implemented and in how healthcare is managed in the new environment. That managed care initiatives would cause such a reaction from physicians should not have come as a surprise. Many physicians believe that managed care is a cost-containment mechanism and that the containment comes through limitation of healthcare services to individuals. Practitioners have an interest in those controls and in whatever changes they bring to bear on their practices and patients.

It serves the healthcare system well if those who must ultimately physically deliver services are involved in the decisions that affect the provision and quality of that care. Be assured, we do not raise the issue of quality as a bludgeon, as physicians in the past have too often been wont to do. There are legitimate cost and practice questions that need to be addressed, but quality is a key part of the discussion. In the interests of good decision making, physicians and other clinical professionals, most notably nurses, need to be equal partners in those discussions. We believe that the product in healthcare is actually the relationship between a patient and a clinician. Clinicians understand that relationship as no nonclinician can.

Thus, the managed care movement, we think, makes physician executives a necessity. Physicians, and other clinicians, will provide the care. It seems obvious that they should have some role in defining, planning, and implementing systems that will make managed care possible and acceptable to clinicians and patients/members alike. Very important, however, the nature of the physician executive's position in the healthcare system is not specified by managed care. At the least, the physician executive will be in charge of clinical practice matters. One presumes that most organizations will want nurses to manage nursing services, financial wizards to manage financial affairs, pharmacists to manage medication systems, etc. As with physicians, there is no inherent need for these individuals to advance in the absence of requisite skill levels, but neither is there any inherent reason for their being held back.

The Forces of Integration

Integration, in its current form, is a relatively new phenomenon. But the notion has an honorable history. The Catholic healthcare systems have historically combined hospitals, nursing homes, and other providers in a single corporate organization. The investor-owned hospital chains that sprouted after the passage of the Medicare/Medicaid legislation sometimes combined an array of provider organizations with insurance mechanisms. Over the past several years, organizations that combine all of these elements and more have been formed in events birthed by the growth of managed care.

Legally and financially, these integrated systems differ widely, from mammoth corporations that own most or all of the elements, to individual units that remain autonomous but contract with the other elements to gain access to "customers." Whether a system is large or small, the effect is largely the same. Control of clinicians' futures through access to patients has at least partially passed from themselves to external decision makers. Their practices are governed by the conditions of the contracts they or others sign with these external elements. And the growing pervasiveness of managed care and of integrated delivery systems makes the likelihood of practicing medicine outside these systems increasingly unlikely.

The drive to integration has encouraged physicians to become involved in management. And it has encouraged those already in management to explore their current positions in terms of future possibilities— and eventualities. Most of the time, the medical directors of two hospitals in the process of merging can expect one of the slots to disappear or to change substantially, often not toward increased or more significant responsibilities. Physician executives will want to have skills for success and to be able to demonstrate them, but they will also want to position themselves for a successful move up or out of their current organization.

As systems grow larger and more complex, what physicians and other clinicians see is a system in which decisions affecting their lives and how they practice will be made at a greater distance and may or may not involve physician input. They want that input, both for themselves and for the profession. Just as important, those who manage the integrated delivery system will want physicians with well-honed management skills to design and implement new clinical delivery systems that meet the exacting demands of providing managed care in an integrated delivery system. A great deal more coordination of clinical services will be required in these integrated delivery systems. Integration requires implementation of new methods of patient care and care management. Success is likely to depend on the active involvement and buy-in of clinicians and physician executives.

A corollary contention of the authors is that physician executives, when they acquire the requisite management knowledge and skills, are uniquely qualified for medical management positions because of their medical training and knowledge. This mirrors the idea that those trained and experienced in financial management are uniquely qualified for comptroller and accountant positions and that those with pharmacy training and backgrounds are uniquely qualified to be chief pharmacists.

What Skills Are Needed?

When physicians first began their return to management roles in the early 1970s, the milieu was medical group practices and the demands were not great. In the beginning, the medical director positions were mostly part time. In many instances, the job simply fell to the most popular or oldest member of the group. The same was true of hospitals when medical directors first began to appear on the scene. The main requirement was a compatible physician whom the medical staff could accept and work with. The goal was to keep the medical staff content and to avoid meaningful involvement of the medical staff in the administration of the organization. A fellow physician seemed the best candidate for the job, and clinical experience was mandatory.

During the past 20 years, we have seen medicine change from a cottage industry to a medical-industrial complex. Physicians were once sole proprietary craftsmen. They produced healthcare services for individuals and managed relatively simple businesses. As medicine began to resemble big business, the role of clinician and business manager split. At first, the business manager was a nonclinician. As the medical-industrial complex firmed, physicians began to see the importance of clinical experience in the decisions made. Thus, the physician executive came into being. As integration succeeds, more complexity will develop as more forces come into play. This will only intensify the need for those with clinical experience in decision-making roles.

The basic set of responsibilities has not changed much, but the environment in which the duties are discharged would be barely recognizable to the medical director of the past. Business is no longer conducted at a fairly leisurely pace in a cost-based reimbursement world in which costs were magically transformed into revenues through third party payors. Those third party payors have long since lost their enthusiasm for that magic act. In managed care operations, revenue centers have become cost centers, and providers and provider organizations have assumed a fuller measure of the business financial risk. The new breed of physician executive must be able to meld business and medicine into a seamless package. To do so, they will have to be extraordinary physicians and extraordinary managers—the former to maintain credibility with an increasingly threatened medical staff, the latter to represent faithfully the interests of physicians in management circles.

While a primary role of physician executives will continue to be to bridge the gap between physicians and organizations, with a foot in each of these camps, they will always have a special allegiance to medicine that those with only management duties will never acquire. This allegiance will also work to the advantage of the healthcare delivery system, because the purpose of the system will continue to be the delivery of healthcare services. It is the system's special purpose that makes the presence of physicians in management roles a desirable outcome. They need not be in a dominant role, but they need to be in a significant one.

The difficulty for physicians interested in management careers has never been associated with learning new skills and knowledge. They are natural learners and committed students. The difficulty, rather, is that traditional medical training and clinical experience are antithetical to management. To succeed as managers, physicians must rigorously assess their styles and make deep, difficult changes. They must be prepared to transform themselves from clinicians to managers by acquiring specific business skills and jettisoning the attitudes that they brought from their clinical backgrounds. It is not a transformation to be taken lightly. Management is not a career change intended to salve the frustrated clinician. It is a positive step that leads a physician to accept more global responsibilities for the direction of healthcare delivery. And once the step into management is taken, a return to clinical practice is never easy and may, with time, become impossible, especially for the procedure-based specialist.

And That's the Dilemma

In physician executive circles, two major dilemmas related to the issue of clinical versus management practice arise:

- Should physicians continue to practice medicine?
- How do physicians fit in the organizational structure?

As we mentioned earlier, many organizations prefer that physicians continue to do the work for which they were trained, that is, practicing medicine. However, it is just this training and experience, the practice of medicine, that makes them valuable in a management capacity. It is important to ask, "How much experience must a physician have to meet the requirement of having clinical experience?" and "What of the physician who stops clinical practice when he or she becomes a manager?" Let us first say that mere training as a physician does not qualify a person as having clinical experience. There are numerous physicians who study business at the same time that they study medicine and graduate with an M.D. or D.O. degree and a business degree, such as an M.B.A. Medical training certainly gives them much more clinical insight than others with only management training. However, the mere presence of M.D. or D.O. behind one's name does not make one a clinician. It is the *type* and *quantity* of the clinical work performed that builds a solid background of clinical experience, as well as the number of years one is in practice. It can be safely said that the longer a physician has been in practice prior to making a shift to management, the more respect he or she will garner among other physicians.

Having said this, let us consider the issue of whether a physician should maintain a clinical practice after the shift to management. Prior to the 1980s, most physician managers maintained at least a token clinical practice as they went about their management duties. Even hospital CEOs and large clinic presidents continued to see patients, at least on occasion. But the demands of management have become more complex, and the systems managed have become broader and more difficult to understand. The body of knowledge required to maintain both clinical and management skills has become so great—and trends appear and change so quickly—that it is very difficult for physicians to maintain knowledge and skills in both management and clinical work. This is especially true for physicians who are in a procedure-based specialty, where the ability to perform a technique begins to atrophy as one performs it less frequently.

Many physician executives are concerned that, if they do not maintain some semblance of a clinical practice, they will no longer be accepted by other physicians as a physician. This brings us to the second aspect of the dilemma. Physicians are notorious for demanding that one of them be involved in decision making; when a physician leaves practice to do just that, however, other physicians may reject that physician as a "turncoat." While maintaining a clinical practice may help a physician to prevent alienation from nonmanagerial physicians, it is very likely that, as physician executives achieve managerial perspective, they will be seen by physicians as no longer being clinicians. While maintaining a clinical practice may help physicians bridge the gap between management and clinician, we do not believe it is the presence or absence of clinical work alone that results in rejection of the physician executive as a turncoat by other physicians. The success of the physician executive in helping clinicians understand and plan for changes and in facilitating accomplishment of the clinicians' goals plays a much larger role in whether the physician is rejected by clinicians.

While the physician executive may be labeled by clinicians as no longer "one of them," he or she is also considered by management as a physician and not a "real" manager. Maintaining a clinical practice may perpetuate this notion among managers. Once again, the success of the physician executive in helping to further organizational goals is more important in how managers perceive the physician executive.

There Has to Be Management Education

Many physicians have completely made the transition to management and left clinical practice behind, and more are poised to do so. This allows them to concentrate their energy on mastering new skills needed for executive positions. To some extent, however, efforts to date have been reactive. Physicians have identified themselves as candidates for management positions, and ACPE and others have offered the requisite education. There have been some efforts to participate in the identification process by promoting the notion of medical management as a career, but more is needed. While physicians are ideal candidates for pure medical management positions, they are also likely candidates for less obvious slots. Medical informatics leaps to mind. The purpose of medical informatics is already a basic part of the physician's skill base, but what is needed is the addition of information technology skills and knowledge. As computer projects such as the electronic medical record and online information become important, clinicians must play a key role in their design and implementation. The healthcare field needs to condition itself to think of physicians in many managerial areas and then work as a unit to ensure that they gain the needed skills. Physicians have already made significant contributions to medical quality management, but they could easily become managers of the full spectrum of allied areas—outcomes management, population-based resource analysis, marketing research, and others. The healthcare system must begin to help clinicians move to new roles of management to capitalize optimally on their knowledge and ability.

Although physicians are this book's special concern, many clinical professionals in healthcare can be tapped for management responsibilities, and the case for other groups is just as persuasive. The healthcare professions are populated by persons of unusually high energy with a dedication to the cause of excellence in the provision of healthcare services. It simply does not make sense not to tap this source of energy for management services. The healthcare field and those professions would gain much from the cross-fertilization.

The work of healthcare is increasingly conducted by teams. Hands-on healthcare requires the services of physicians, nurses, pharmacists, therapists, technicians, technologists, and many more. Their ministrations must be augmented by the expertise of dietitians, housekeepers, and numerous other ancillary service personnel. And the whole healthcare enterprise requires the attention of a cadre of specialist and generalist managers. Especially in an integrated managed care world, the fiefdom view of operations is no longer effective—if it ever was. New and increased stresses caused by structural changes have simply forced the issue. Conditions and directions cannot be successfully dictated by any single collection of these professionals. Administrators and physicians often undertake, and quarrel about, these responsibilities, with the other actors largely "going along" or carping from the edges. The new healthcare system design will require a far more meaningful sharing of responsibility in a team-oriented environment. Antagonisms and differences will not disappear, of course, but they will have to be addressed through collaboration and cooperation, not fiat and resistance.

There will be leaders in such a system, of course, and that is where we believe physicians can play an important role. A critical implementation role for healthcare managers in the future will be identifying potential leaders in the ranks of teams, providing them with the skills needed to lead and manage healthcare activities, and elevating them to system responsibilities as they demonstrate the required competence. The business of healthcare will remain health services. Physicians and other clinicians have a special competence that, augmented by management training, will ensure that the healthcare system does not fall prey to the same financial traps that Halberstam claims nearly doomed the U.S. auto industry. The danger in any enterprise, as Halberstam (1986) pointed out, is management's thinking that the purpose of the enterprise is to make money. That is a necessary outcome, but excellence of product or service is the purpose. Physicians, because they are a key component of the provider-patient relationship, know a great deal about that purpose for the healthcare system.

In the remainder of this book, some leading experts and commentators on the U.S. healthcare system expand on the issues raised in this chapter. Joel Shalowitz, M.D., of Northwestern University provides a more extensive view of the current state of the healthcare system and of medicine. His views lay the foundation for the premise of this book that physicians have a crucial role in healthcare management. He also begins the discussion of team approaches to the delivery and management of care. This is a key issue, for it draws our attention away from the notion of squabbling healthcare professions and toward a notion of teamwork and equality. In this latter view, any professional can, given the resources and capabilities, rise to a top management position.

Deborah Shlian, M.D., draws a picture of the current state of medical management and the forces that encourage and impede the development of physician executives. Dr. Shlian draws on her extensive experience as an executive recruiter—monitoring the expectations of healthcare organizations and working with physicians to ensure that they acquire and effectively demonstrate the desired skills. She clearly shares our enthusiasm for physicians in management roles.

Jay Noren, M.D., M.P.H., and David Kindig, M.D., Ph.D., of the University of Wisconsin, add immeasurably to the discussion of what skills and credentials a physician ought to bring to the medical management market. Management is no easy matter. The skills required are complex and demanding. The authors make a strong case for rigorously acquiring management education and training, suggesting that having such credentials will prove more and more valuable as the competition for medical management positions heats up and as physicians become increasingly interested in top executive positions.

Sandra Gill takes our comments on the transition from clinical practice to management and both explores the pitfalls and how to avoid them. She is mindful that success in this transition is not guaranteed and that much of a physician's education and training mitigates against success. She also goes into greater detail on the proper balance between clinical practice and management at various stages of a physician's move to management.

Mark Doyne, M.D., in a personal and anecdotal fashion, describes what it takes to succeed in medical management. His advice gets directly at the core competencies that the physician executive needs and at the political factors that have to be considered in the job-seeking process. Medical management, Dr. Doyne strongly implies, is not for the faint at heart.

Kenneth Cummings, M.D., raises what we believe is a key issue for the healthcare field as it moves more completely to managed care and as now-independent components increasingly become parts of integrated systems. These changes are occurring rapidly, a situation that can easily lead to distrust and resistance. Clinicians generally are under siege at a time that requires more teamwork than ever before. It is not a natural environment for trusting relationships, but Dr. Cummings makes a strong case for exactly that. All the parties to the effort will need to work hard on trust if the overall effort is to succeed. And he shows how trusting relationships can be developed, even in difficult times.

And that leads naturally to the chapter by Roger Battistella, Ph.D., and Thomas Weil, Ph.D., on the linkages between clinician and nonclinician roles in the healthcare system. As we have moved from cottage industry to medical-industrial complex, physicians are no longer the only key part of the healthcare system. The fast-moving and constantly changing system will require leaders and workers who understand the need for teamwork. And teams will also change as needs change. If caregivers are to share their natural allegiance to patients with a new allegiance to an organization happily, those who manage the organization will need a keen understanding of the original allegiance. Others can acquire such an understanding, but clinicians are a step ahead.

Finally, Montague Brown, Dr.P.H., takes a look into the future to see where all the relationships discussed in this book can be expected to evolve. Making such a forecast is a risky undertaking, but Dr. Brown brings many years' exposure to the healthcare delivery system to the task.

References

AHA Guide to the Health Care Field, 1986. 1986. Chicago: American Hospital Association.

AHA Guide to the Health Care Field, 1996. 1997. Chicago: American Hospital Association.

American College of Physician Executives (ACPE) membership database. 1997. Tampa, FL: ACPE.

Halberstam, D. 1986. *The Reckoning.* New York: William Morrow and Company.

Kushner, J. 1995. *Preparing to Tack: When Physicians Change Careers.* New York: Vantage Press.

Nash, D. (ed.). 1993. *Future Practice Alternatives in Medicine,* 2nd ed. New York: Igaku-Shoin.

Neuhauser, D. 1983. *Coming of Age: A 50-Year History of the American College of Hospital Administrators and the Profession It Serves, 1933–1983.* Chicago: American College of Healthcare Executives.

Physician Characteristics and Distribution in the U.S. 1997. Chicago: American Medical Association.

Starr, P. 1982. *The Social Transformation of American Medicine.* New York: Basic Books.

The Healthcare System and Medicine— Current States

Joel Shalowitz

THE STRUCTURE of our healthcare system is, in large part, caused by the financial incentives we created to pay for its services and products. The traditional payment system is responsible for fragmenting the healthcare we provide, causing many of our quality and cost problems. Organized delivery systems and managed care plans emerged as responses to these problems and have attempted to organize care across a continuum of services, and this change from fragmentation to integration requires the cooperation of practicing clinicians and their nonclinical colleagues.

This chapter reviews the current status of healthcare financing in this country and some of its major problems. An introduction to some basic principles of insurance is presented first, followed by a discussion of the historical development of private and public health insurance. The following section reviews managed care. Finally, some thoughts are presented about the future status of health insurance coverage.

Basic Principles of Insurance

There are two reasons for beginning this chapter with a discussion of insurance principles. First, we need a reference point to gauge how far we have come (or strayed) from the basic purposes of insurance. Second, in light of (or in spite of) these principles, we must understand what people expect from their coverage (Anonymous 1988).

Insurance products were created for two reasons: to protect policy holders against catastrophic losses and to give them the ability to budget for the expenses associated with that protection. Unfortunately, with respect to health insurance, we have often violated both of these principles. While many well-intentioned public interest groups have lobbied for inclusion of such valuable health services as appropriate screening tests and immunizations, other benefits, such as those related to infertility (including in vitro fertilization), cross the line from necessary medical and public health measures to personal interest lobbying. We have thus moved far from the notion of insuring only catastrophic risk.

Being able to budget for health insurance has also become increasingly difficult. Rapidly rising health insurance costs during the 1970s and 1980s forced large businesses to switch from traditional indemnity insurance to managed care products. Further, in areas such as Minneapolis and Cleveland, businesses formed coalitions that demanded large discounts from local healthcare providers. Other large purchasers, such as the California Public Employees' Retirement System (CalPERS), have also demanded and received discounts from managed care companies. However, small employers, individuals whose employers do not provide coverage, and the self-employed are still subject to uncertain costs.

Despite the recent stabilization in large employer healthcare costs, two impediments remain for the *individual* who wants to budget for health insurance. First, in addition to moderating premiums, large employers are paying less for their health insurance because they are shifting more of the burden of payment to employees and covering fewer family members. Second, even if overall healthcare costs are currently restrained, it is only a temporary phenomenon. The major reason for rising healthcare costs is the rapid implementation of technology. Unfortunately, the approach to solving this problem has been piecemeal. Programs such as the Blue Cross/Blue Shield Medical Necessity Project and the Clinical Efficacy Assessment Project of the American College of Physicians have contributed to our understanding of the efficacy and effectiveness of technology. Little has been done on a larger scale, however, to implement, monitor, and continuously improve these recommendations. Further, the federal government has failed to support centralized, coordinated technology assessment. In fact, the policy has recently been quite the opposite: In September 1995, Congress eliminated the Office of Technology Assessment. More recently, funding for the Agency for Health Care Policy and Research has been greatly jeopardized. In light of these recent congressional actions, as well as the lobbying of many special interest groups, it is unlikely that we will have a coordinated, comprehensive national technology assessment program in the near future. To compound the problem, states continue to expand their mandates that insurers cover specific high-technology services, such as the infertility services mentioned above.

Conditions for Insurance

Traditional indemnity insurance principles dictate that to be insurable an occurrence must have these characteristics: First, the event must happen with some regularity but not occur very frequently or too rarely. Obviously, if the event occurred too frequently, the cost of purchasing insurance would be close to the total replacement cost of the sustained loss. If the occurrence is too rare, one would not even be interested in paying a very small amount for protection.

Second, the incident must occur randomly and unpredictably. A corollary is that the episode must be beyond the control of the insured (the issue of "moral hazard"). Several features of typical health insurance policies in this country violate this principle: Preventive services (such as immunizations) and screening (such as mammography) are frequently covered. While they are appropriate public health and medical measures and their provision undoubtedly saves money, strictly speaking, they do not meet the definition of insurable services. Further, some conditions are covered in this country because of decisions we, as a society, have decided to make. For example, most health insurance policies cover pregnancy. This condition is not covered by many insurance plans in, for example, Japan, because Japanese society does not view pregnancy as a random and unpredictable event. Cultural differences in healthcare benefits exist in other countries as well. For example, spa care is a traditional health benefit in Germany. These cultural differences highlight the fact that we cover some services for strictly social reasons. Finally, some states have recently proposed that insurance companies must accept insured persons at any time, regardless of their health status. These proposals come without the simultaneous requirement that all people have coverage. Critics of this proposal correctly liken it to requiring a company to offer fire insurance to a homeowner while his house is burning down. These proposals clearly violate the principle of unpredictability.

Third, despite the issues of frequency and unpredictability, the frequency and cost of the event must be estimable. A corollary is that the cost of the loss must have a nontrivial value; otherwise, no one would be willing to buy insurance.

Finally, in providing insurance, the insurer requires large numbers of subscribers to make sufficient and regular payments (premiums). The smaller the number of those insured, the greater the risk for the insurer and the greater the premium the company must demand to shield itself from risk. This principle has ever-increasing importance for healthcare providers because acceptance of capitation converts the provider into an insurance company. It is also difficult to negotiate prices without being able to estimate the volume of services to be provided.

What Consumers Want from Their Insurance Plans

The word *consumer* means both those who use healthcare and those who pay for it. Therefore, it includes such parties as potential patients and their employers. Table 2.1 lists the features that consumers want from their insurance plans. This list is based on numerous unpublished interviews by the author.

The first principle is one of access—that is, the insured must first be able to obtain insurance. Because the number of uninsured has grown to about 40 million, this feature is not trivial.

Second, consumers want the highest quality of care. Often, however, the quality they desire is not related to the price they wish to pay. Regardless of cost issues, many organizations (such as the National Committee on Quality Assurance, the Foundation for Accountability, and the Joint Commission on Accreditation of Healthcare Organizations) are surveying health plans for quality measures along structural, process, and outcome dimensions. While in many respects this scrutiny is laudable, it often presents a large administrative burden on providers of care, particularly if they contract with multiple health plans.

Unlike the case with quality, when consumers want a rich benefits package, they realize they *do* have to pay for what they get. Some benefits, such as pharmaceuticals and eyeglasses, can be options in a traditional policy. Others, like the state-mandated benefits mentioned above, must

Table 2.1 What Consumers Want from Their Insurance Plans

- Access to insurance
- High-quality care
- Comprehensive benefits
- Ease of administration
- Low premiums
- First-dollar coverage
- Freedom to choose providers

be offered to all non-ERISA-exempt purchasers, even if they do not want them. This situation, of course, raises the cost of health insurance. Fortunately for consumers, many health plans—particularly managed care plans—have competed in recent years by enhancing the scope of benefits they provide for the same cost. This latter trend, however, may have already peaked.

Ease of administration concerns such member services as eligibility verification, complaint resolution, minimization of paperwork, and claims payment. While many health plans are variably successful in each of these activities, state and federal laws are now forcing them to enhance their efficiency. For example, federal regulations for Medicare managed care beneficiaries now set limits on times to resolve denied referrals and pay claims.

The final three features are inextricably linked: If one were to get more in one dimension, one would have to give something up in one or both of the other two. For example, with benefits held constant, the lowest premiums and highest first-dollar coverage (that is, out-of-pocket expenses) occur with traditional capitated health maintenance organizations (HMOs). What one surrenders, however, is complete freedom to choose one's providers. Likewise, if one wishes more freedom to choose providers and still wants low premiums, out-of-pocket expenses will be higher in the form of deductibles, coinsurance, and copayments. Such is the case with preferred provider organizations (PPOs) and point-of-service (POS) plans. The greatest freedom to choose providers, of course, occurs in the traditional indemnity market; however, compared to the previously mentioned managed care products, total costs in the form of premiums and out-of-pocket expenses can be much higher. Providers who contract with health plans offering low premiums, low out-of-pocket expenses, and a great deal of freedom to choose providers are taking a risk because of the doubtful financial viability of those programs. Likewise, providers who accept capitation under these circumstances must gauge whether they have sufficient control over referrals in deciding whether these rates are adequate.

The features employers consider when choosing a health plan can, in part, be found in Figure 2.1. While these findings represent the consensus of all the businesses surveyed, there is a major dichotomy between what large companies (those with 500 to 1,000 employees) and small firms want from their health insurance. The large companies, having already negotiated lower prices through their market power, consider quality factors far more important than price. Small employers, on the other hand, who do not have any leverage over insurance plans, consider price the most important factor in choosing their insurance. As the

Figure 2.1 Information Employers Use to Select Health Plans (Top and Bottom 5 Sources of 22 Survey Information Categories)

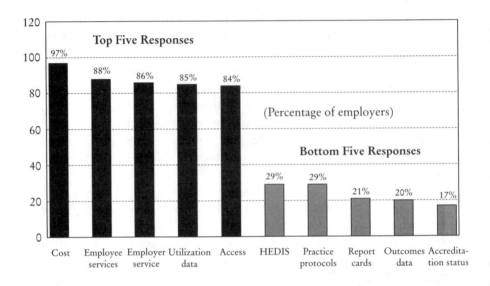

Source: Washington Business Group on Health/Watson Wyatt Worldwide employer survey, 1996

marketplace consolidates, and more plans look to small- and medium-size employers as their customers, prices will probably moderate, and plans will compete on the basis of the benefits they offer and of valid, reliable, and statistically significant quality measures they can demonstrate.

Private Health Insurance

The way we currently view health insurance and what we expect from its coverage are rooted in history. Therefore, in order to understand our present system, it is important to appreciate the impact of some key historical events and landmark legislation. A current estimate of the distribution of our insured population by type of coverage is contained in Figure 2.2.

Our present system of insurance has its origins in the European guilds, which collected money from members and paid benefits to workers' families upon their death or disability. Because medical and surgical care were primitive, of relatively low cost, and of brief duration, payments for these services were practically nonexistent. In this country, similar coverage began to emerge in the mid-nineteenth century. Instead of trade guilds, organizations were formed by members with common religious,

Figure 2.2   How Americans Are Insured (1996 Enrollment, in Millions)

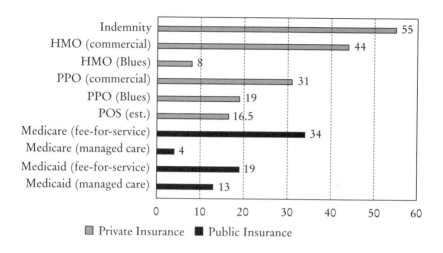

Sources: Foster Higgins, Health Insurance Association of America, Blue Cross–Blue Shield Assn., Employee Benefits Research Institute, Health Care Financing Administration, Kaiser Family Foundation

ethnic, or national backgrounds. By the late-nineteenth century, associations emerged at the workplace that were initiated by employees, employees and employers, and—rarely—solely by employers. The main purpose of these associations was to furnish cash payments for disability and death; medical benefits were rarely provided. Of note is that these organizations often hired physicians to provide advice and certification of disability. Thus, the use of physicians as gatekeepers originated more than a century ago; patients were not eligible for benefits unless a physician certified their disability. As the associations' benefits began to incorporate medical care, they hired doctors on a prepaid basis to attend to their members. Contrary to popular belief, therefore, capitation is not a new phenomenon associated with HMOs. An early example of this type of payment was the Pacific Railway Beneficial Association (begun in 1882).

The latter part of the nineteenth century saw the emergence of the labor union movement. The benefits that unions provided mirrored those of the European guilds; initially only disability and death assistance were provided. Several decades passed before they offered medical benefits.

With the beginning of the twentieth century came employer-sponsored health insurance. In 1910, Montgomery Ward and Company replaced its "employee establishment fund" with an insured contract, an event generally regarded as the first group health policy. By the 1920s, more companies had their health insurance plans underwritten by commercial insurers. Not all types of healthcare benefits emerged simultaneously. During the 1930s, hospital expense insurance was the first type of coverage to become prevalent. Later, payment for care by a surgeon emerged. It was not until the early 1940s that nonsurgical medical care was commonly reimbursed. The reason for the development of coverage in this order is obvious: It followed the higher cost and potentially catastrophic nature of illnesses that could be treated by existing technology.

Like the rest of the country in the 1930s, hospitals faced precarious financial positions. To ensure a steady cash flow and to minimize delinquent accounts, individual hospitals established their own insurance programs. One of the first such programs was established in 1929 at Baylor Hospital. While these hospital programs benefited their sponsors, individual state insurance commissions were concerned that plan subscribers had limited freedom to choose institutions and that geographic coverage was limited. To help solve this problem, the American Hospital Association facilitated in 1933 the formation of multihospital insurance programs in states. In exchange for allowing these programs to develop, the state insurance commissioners required that these plans be not-for-profit, have their premiums regulated at community rates, and be open to enrollment to the general population. These statewide multihospital plans were the origins of the current Blue Cross system. Similar programs to cover physicians' fees developed simultaneously across the country and were the forerunners of Blue Shield plans. Of note is that the American Hospital Association severed its relationship with Blue Cross in 1972, about the same time that the Blue Cross organization merged with the national Blue Shield association.

Along with their not-for-profit status, Blue Cross plans were regulated like utilities; for example, they were unable to raise rates without insurance commission permission and could not engage in risk underwriting. Competing commercial insurance plans, therefore, chose the lowest risk accounts and underbid the Blue Cross plans. As a result of this competition, such plans were losing significant membership by the 1970s. Blue Cross has only recently allowed its members to convert to for-profit status to compete more effectively in the health insurance marketplace. This conversion trend has gained momentum and has resulted in the establishment of not-for-profit foundations worth billions of dollars. As of mid-1997, total enrollment in the 58 different Blues plans totaled 68.6 million members.

More than 150 million Americans now receive their health insurance through their employers. The impetus for the change from individual, noncorporate purchase to these employer-sponsored plans had its origins during and shortly after World War II. Several conditions led to this change. First, when men enlisted or were drafted into the military, their health insurance was assumed by the federal government. Their families therefore lost private coverage. Second, employers recognized that health benefits were important to the wives of servicemen who sought employment and offered them policies to attract qualified workers. Third, because of the wage and price freezes during World War II, employers were able to offer these benefits in lieu of higher salaries. Finally, subsequent changes in the Internal Revenue Service tax code made these benefits tax deductible for the employer and tax exempt for the employee. This change created a subsidy for the purchase of health insurance.

It is important to note that this tax subsidy is the third largest federally financed health program (after Medicare and Medicaid), representing an implicit cost of more than $40 billion per year (Iglehart 1992). Since initiation of this tax exemption, there has been considerable debate about the continuance of the subsidy. Opponents of its termination argue that it is another way for the government to increase taxes while potentially causing hardship to some employers and employees. Proponents for its elimination claim that the tax exemption insulates purchasers from the real costs of healthcare and prevents them from becoming prudent buyers. Although this debate will undoubtedly continue, it is unlikely this tax subsidy will be eliminated in the near future.

With regard to commercial health insurance, one of the most significant events of the past 50 years was passage of the Employee Retirement and Income Security Act (ERISA) in 1974. The purpose of this act was to ensure that workers entitled to private pension benefits actually received them. Section 514, however, allowed employers to establish self-funded health insurance plans that were exempt from state laws pertaining to mandated benefits. Over half of all persons insured through their employers are covered under these types of plans. The advantages to self-insurance are listed in Table 2.2.

Of particular concern for policymakers and the public has been the exemption from state-mandated benefits, which have ranged from preventive services to hairpieces for chemotherapy patients. It has been estimated that the costs of these mandates can add at least 4 to 5 percent to insurance premiums. ERISA plans can claim exemptions from these mandates because the law is a federal statute that takes precedence over insurance regulations of the individual states. Although recent court cases have been settled in favor of states that sought to require these plans

Table 2.2 Advantages to Employer of Self-Insurance under ERISA

- Exemption from state insurance premium tax (typically 2 to 3 percent)
- Exemption from state-mandated benefits
- Exemption from financing reserve requirements
- Exemption from contributions to state risk pools
- Full access to claims data
- Ability to pay claims after they are received, which gives employers the ability to "play the float" on reserves
- Exemption from broker commissions
- Ability to standardize benefits across all locations for multistate companies

to pay local hospital surcharges, ERISA protection is still formidable. Many healthcare policymakers still think that there will be no meaningful national health reform without substantial federal revision or repeal of ERISA.

At this point, it is important to mention briefly the regulation of health insurance. Each state has a department of insurance that oversees its own health insurance plans. At the national level is the National Association of Insurance Commissioners (NAIC), whose members are the state insurance commissioners. The NAIC recommends legal and regulatory initiatives to standardize the insurance industry. Of significance, however, is that this body has no power to implement or enforce its recommendations. Thus, for traditional, private indemnity insurance, regulatory powers reside at the state level.

Another important health insurance law, the Consolidated Omnibus Reconciliation Act (COBRA), passed in 1985, enables workers and their dependents to extend their group healthcare coverage when the covered person loses benefits due to such events as termination from employment, death, divorce, or separation from a spouse. Although this act allows continued access to health insurance, the employer is no longer obligated to pay its portion of the premium; the beneficiary must therefore pay the entire cost of the policy plus an additional 2 percent administration fee. The ability to continue coverage under this policy is time-limited according to the circumstances that enabled its purchase. For example, there is 36-month maximum coverage for surviving spouses and dependent children who lose their coverage as a result of the death of an employee.

The most recent major legislative change was the Health Insurance Portability and Accountability Act (the so-called Kennedy-Kassebaum Law), which was passed in 1996. The general intent of this law was to enable workers to change jobs without the threat of losing health insurance because of a preexisting condition. It does not, however, guarantee insurance for those whose new employer does not provide health benefits, nor does it guarantee waiver of any waiting periods if an employee comes from a setting that did not provide such insurance. A more experimental part of that act is a provision allowing the establishment of medical savings accounts (MSAs), which would be available for a limited number of people who work for companies with 50 or fewer employees. Advocates of MSAs claim they would force consumers to be more cost-sensitive in purchasing healthcare, while opponents contend that only the healthy would choose this option. The remainder of the population, therefore, would be sicker and would raise premium rates for all.

Public Programs

The major publicly funded programs include Medicare, Medicaid, the Veterans Administration System, care for the active military and their dependents (CHAMPUS), and public health programs. Only Medicare and Medicaid will be discussed here. For a more detailed discussion of background and statistics for these programs as well as their benefits, the reader should consult the Internet home page for the Health Care Financing Administration at http://www.hcfa.gov/medicare/medmed.htm (Friedman 1995). The purpose of Medicare was and is to increase eligible members' access to care by removing financial barriers. Medicare has two parts.

Medicare Part A

The major expenses paid by the Part A Trust Fund are inpatient hospital expenses, skilled nursing home care, and home health visits. The source of funding for these services is a 1.45 percent payroll tax that the employer and employee each pay (the self-employed pay 2.9 percent). In recent years, the differences between program revenue and program expenses have been narrowing. By 1996, expenses started to exceed revenues. The federal government now predicts that the fund will be in a deficit position by 2001. Current budget proposals to ensure fiscal solvency of this fund beyond that time are focused on cutting payments to providers (such as physicians, hospitals, skilled care facilities and home health agencies) and to contracted administrators (such as HMOs). As history has shown, however, cutting payments is only a short-term solution. Major reforms in the way we pay for care, how healthcare services are delivered, and who receives coverage are needed to ensure long-term solvency of the plan. Such changes could include a global payment by episode of illness, competitive bidding by systems of care to deliver services to the elderly, and extension of the eligible age from 65 to at least 67.

The Medicare fund has faced bankruptcy in the past as a result of uncontrolled spending and flawed reimbursement methods. When the Medicare program began operations in 1966, it offered hospitals payment on a cost-plus basis. This enticement was used to ensure widespread participation among providers. Included in reimbursable costs were expenses attributable to capital investments, such as interest payments on bonds used for building expansion. Medicare thus became a major factor in hospital facility expansion over the past three decades. When expenses rose rapidly, Medicare changed payment to a cost-basis. Hospitals, however, were able to allocate much of their indirect expenses to Medicare patients and still reap substantial financial benefit. Furthermore, the federal government paid hospitals monthly, based on a moving average of past payments. The resulting regular cash flow became very important to these institutions. Periodic reconciliations were made to account for actual services provided.

When the cost-based system also resulted in projected deficits, Congress passed the Tax Equity and Fiscal Responsibility Act of 1982 (TEFRA). The first, and most immediate, effect of this law was on cash flow: With abolition of the system of periodic interim payments to hospitals and implementation of a diagnosis-related group (DRG) method (a global payment by disease category), hospitals had to submit claims individually to get paid.

The second effect was that this new payment system caused increased tensions between physicians and hospitals, principally in three areas:

- Medicare reimbursement incentives for hospitals and physicians began to conflict. Prior to implementation of DRGs, the longer the patient was in the hospital and the more services the physician ordered, the more both hospital and physician were paid. Under DRGs, hospitals are paid a single amount based on the patient's principal admitting diagnosis. Physicians, on the other hand, continue to be paid on a daily rate. Under this system, the longer the patient is in the hospital, the higher physician reimbursement is; hospital profitability, on the other hand, will fall.

- Because hospitals need to submit bills in a timely fashion to receive reimbursement, they require physicians to complete medical records accurately and promptly. Because physicians submit their own bills separately from the hospitals, there is no financial incentive for them to complete their charting on a timely basis.

- To protect themselves from potential lawsuits, physicians may order tests that are not medically necessary. These tests are free to physicians but the hospital must pay for them from its DRG reimbursement.

The third major result of passage of TEFRA was the enabling legislation for Medicare HMOs. More will be said about these types of plans below.

Finally, the DRG system had a profound impact on health costs for indemnity plans. Because DRGs resulted in decreased Medicare payments, many hospitals raised their prices for private payors in a process called *cost shifting*. These rate increases were one major reason for rapidly rising commercial health insurance premiums. Many businesses reacted to these higher premiums either by becoming self-insured or by actively seeking managed care products.

Medicare Part B

The principal services and products for which Medicare Part B pays are physician care and durable medical equipment. Financing for this portion of Medicare comes from three sources. About three quarters of the funding comes from general tax revenues. Traditionally, about 25 percent has come from beneficiaries, although this percentage has been decreasing in recent years. A small percentage of the Part B budget comes from the interest on the Part A Trust Fund. While both Medicare Parts A and B are entitlements for which one is automatically eligible at age 65, unlike Part A, Part B is voluntary. One must, however, actively disenroll in Part B in order not to receive its benefits. Disenrollment occurs primarily among individuals who are working past age 65 and are covered by their employers' health plan. Medicare Part B would, in these circumstances, be redundant coverage for them. It is appropriate to note here that private insurance is always primary over Medicare. The one exception is specifically designated Medicare supplements.

With regard to physician payments, Medicare fees were initially based on a usual, customary, and reasonable (UCR) schedule called "customary, prevailing, and reasonable" fees. These amounts were originally determined by such factors as geography; whether the physician was in solo or group practice; and, in the case of the nonsurgical specialties, whether the physician was a specialist or subspecialist. This schedule had all of the problems of the UCR system (Roe 1981). Because of rising payments, a different methodology was sought. A resource-based relative value scale (RBRVS) proposed by Hsiao et al. (1988) was chosen. Currently, it includes a total work component and a geography-based measure of specialty-practice costs. The RBRVS schedule has also been adopted by many commercial insurers, who pay physicians based on a percentage at, above, or below these fees.

Despite this relatively recent change, this component of Medicare Part B still has problems. First, the total work component was based on historical fees, not actual marketplace charges. Therefore, the starting base was higher than it could have been. For example, in the mid-1980s in the Chicago area, Medicare reimbursement to ophthalmologists for cataract removal with lens implant was $1,800. Some commercial health plans (including HMOs), on the other hand, were paying $1,100 to $1,200. Recent updates in the fee schedule have taken this historical factor into account and substantially reduced payments to surgical specialties. Second, this type of system fails to recognize that total healthcare costs are a function not only of prices but also of volume and intensity of services. While the federal government originally intended to use volume-performance standards in updating the RBRVS schedule, such explicit adjustments have not been forthcoming. As a matter of fact, some changes have been surprising. The financial incentives of RBRVS were intended to reward cognitive services and reduce payments for procedures. When the growth in surgical services was reduced and the growth in medical services rose (as one would expect if the goals of this system were being met), surgeons were rewarded with an increased update factor (a percentage multiplier) in their fees, while primary care physicians had much smaller increases. (Smaller increases, or decreases, in surgical fees have been the rule more recently.)

Finally, fee schedules do not control for physician-initiated substitution of more complex procedures for simpler ones or more rapid introduction of newer technology, both of which raise costs for Part B services. In considering intensity of service issues, one also cannot exclude the possibility that many physicians may be inappropriately "upcoding" to increase reimbursement for their services.

Medicaid

The Medicaid Program is a joint federal-state initiative. Although federal standards set general eligibility parameters for participation that are based on financial criteria and types of services that must be offered, large variations exist from state to state across both these dimensions. A brief explanation of eligibility, scope of services, financial issues and recent managed care initiatives will be presented below. For more details, one should consult the HCFA web page.

Unlike Medicare, which is a standard federal program for which recipients become automatically eligible at age 65, one must apply for

Medicaid in one's state of residence. Because many eligible recipients never apply and many others go on and off the rolls, it is difficult to calculate how many potential beneficiaries exist. There are three basic categories of persons eligible for Medicaid benefits. First is the so-called "mandatory group." These persons must be included in Medicaid programs if the state wants to receive federal funds. A second category is the "objectional group." A state *may* provide benefits for those in this group and receive a contribution of federal funds to care for them. The last category is "optional state programs." The state may provide certain benefits for these recipients; however, the federal government will not provide any additional payment for them. The key financial criterion for eligibility has been recipients' financial status relative to the federal poverty level. The cutoff percentage over this level has varied in the past.

For a state to receive federal funding, it must provide a specified set of services. The states may also offer optional services for which the federal government will help pay. It is noteworthy, however, that there is extreme variability in the *extent* of coverage for each of the mandated services. For example, states must provide hospital and outpatient care, but the number of days and visits can vary substantially from state to state. Many states have found, however, that providing optional services will actually save money rather than result in additional net expenditures. For example, although pharmaceuticals are not a mandatory benefit under federal guidelines, states have discovered that, if they do not provide prescription drugs to recipients, their healthcare costs will increase.

As mentioned above, costs of the Medicaid program are shared between the federal government and each state. The formula used to calculate the state's share is: state dollar contribution = (average state per capita income/national per capita income) × 45 percent. The problem with this formula is that it uses *averages* rather than relying on the *total number* of poor people who could potentially benefit from the program.

Given this financial responsibility, several payment issues are noteworthy. First, states can set their own rate payment structures. Because of rapidly rising costs, however, states have been reducing the amounts they pay providers and increasing the time in which they make those payments. Although recent court cases and federal law (the so-called Boren Amendment) have mandated that payment be timely and reasonable, those terms have been subject to varying interpretation. Second, this mandate is particularly important because providers must accept Medicaid fees as payment in full and cannot balance bill patients. Finally, when a Medicaid recipient is also eligible for Medicare benefits, the latter coverage is primary and Medicaid pays any Medicare premiums and deductibles.

A major inequity in Medicaid is the financial allocation to eligible populations. The largest eligible group (in terms of numbers) is in the category of aid to families with dependent children (AFDC). The other major category is the aged, blind, and disabled (ABD). Included in this latter category are those for whom Medicaid is the principal source of funding for their nursing home care. While AFDC recipients constitute approximately 70 percent of all Medicaid eligibles, only about 30 percent of payments are for services to those beneficiaries. The large discrepancy between funding for those in the AFDC category and the ABD group is caused by nursing home expenses. Attempts to correct this variance have met with resistance from organizations lobbying on behalf of nursing home residents and their families. These groups have demonstrated more political prowess than the women and children who share Medicaid funding. Greater public advocacy is needed for this latter group, particularly given the impending rapid rise in the elderly population because of increased longevity and baby boomer aging.

Cost increases in the Medicaid program resulted from changes in price, volume, and intensity of services. With regard to price, Medicaid programs have had to pay more because of the aforementioned court cases and of legislation mandating adequate compensation for services. Volume considerations have manifested themselves in both the aging of the population (and hence increased requirements for long-term care funding) and an increase in the size of the nonelderly Medicaid-eligible population. In this latter category are those who are new to poverty as well as recipients who became eligible through additional federal mandates for coverage. Finally, application of higher technology procedures (particularly those in the neonatology arena) have increased Medicaid expenditures.

In an attempt to stem rising Medicaid costs, many states have turned to managed care programs (Rowland and Hanson 1996; Gold, Sparer, and Chu 1996). For a state to implement a Medicaid managed care program, it must obtain a waiver from the federal government. This waiver allows a state to develop funding and delivery systems other than those mandated by the traditional Medicaid regulations. Two types of waivers exist. A Section 1915(b) Waiver allows states to require Medicaid beneficiaries to enroll in managed care plans or to implement managed care programs in only part of the state or for certain categories of beneficiaries. As of September 1995, 42 states and the District of Columbia had this type of waiver. A Section 1115 Waiver (also called a research and demonstration waiver) permits statewide Medicaid demonstration projects that do not meet federal statutory requirements. These programs allow states to shift Medicaid recipients into mandatory managed care programs, enroll them in plans serving predominantly Medicaid recipients, and expand coverage to low-income individuals and families not currently eligible. Approximately ten such programs now exist.

Although implementation of these waiver programs has been credited with a reduction in state Medicaid costs, several problems have arisen. First, not all states have adequate enrollment, marketing, and eligibility systems to ensure recipients a smooth transition into managed care programs. Second, many states do not have adequate oversight programs to handle complaints from these newly enrolled members. Third, while payment methods can vary widely (from individual specialty capitation to putting primary care physicians at risk for paying specialists), these amounts are often not risk-adjusted. Considering the health status of these populations, this flaw can put a severe financial burden on physicians and other providers. Fourth, in some waiver programs benefits are fragmented. This problem arises when the state "carves out" some services from its managed care benefits and allows recipients to access the traditional Medicaid system to receive them. For example, in some states, whole categories (for example, pediatrics) are separated from the waiver program and are delivered through traditional Medicaid. This fragmentation confuses recipients and can lead to uncoordinated care for entire families. Fifth, enrolling large numbers of members in a relatively short time, combined with a shortage of providers, can cause massive confusion and program breakdown. This situation was particularly noteworthy in TennCare, the Tennessee program. Additionally, even when the number of providers is adequate, patients may not have easy access to them, because of transportation and geographic problems, for example.

Although many problems still exist with waivered plans, states have seen them as the solution to their rapidly rising Medicaid costs. They also prefer these plans to block grants that have been proposed from time to time by the federal government. It is therefore likely that more waivered programs will be introduced in the future.

Managed Care

The term *managed care* has been applied to a variety of health insurance products. What they all have in common is some type of utilization review and varying degrees of formal contracting relationships with healthcare providers. The three typical organizations commonly associated with managed care are PPOs, HMOs, and relatively newer hybrids of the two, often called POS plans.

PPOs

The specific operational features of PPOs vary significantly. They do, however, share four characteristics. First, the insurer contracts with a panel of providers. Second, these providers agree to a negotiated fee schedule. As stated above, the current basis for this schedule is usually a percentage of RBRVS. Third, providers agree to abide by a specified utilization review process. Finally, plan members can see any physician in or out of the contracted network and still have some of the bill paid by the insurer. Members will have lower out-of-pocket expenses if they see contracted providers than if noncontracted ones are consulted.

POS Plans

In this type of plan, payment mechanisms and incentives vary so widely that precise characterization is not possible. For example, plans characterizing themselves as POS products may or may not capitate physicians and may or may not share in the cost savings with them. The most that can be said is that they are a hybrid of an HMO and a PPO.

HMOs

An HMO is a healthcare plan that delivers comprehensive, coordinated medical service to voluntarily enrolled members on a prepaid basis. Several aspects of this definition require further explanation. First is the word *comprehensive.* HMOs have historically provided more extensive benefits than has traditional indemnity insurance. Further, they have provided these benefits on a community-rated basis rather than on an individual risk-adjusted one. More recently, with changes in insurance law, HMOs have been allowed to price these benefits on more of a risk-adjusted premium scale.

A second key feature of HMOs is that care is coordinated by the patient's primary care physician, usually an internist, family practitioner, or pediatrician. Although this coordination has sometimes been pejoratively called a "gatekeeper function," the author believes this feature is responsible for the enhanced quality and cost savings that many studies have found in HMO plans compared to their indemnity counterparts. Current legislation in many states is undermining this concept by enabling patients enrolled in traditional HMOs to seek specialty care without approval of a primary care physician. (While such freedom was always an option, these laws now require plans to pay for unreferred services.) The reason for passage of such legislation is to give patients more freedom of choice and to combat alleged inappropriate withholding of referrals by primary care physicians. Although the popular press has publicized individual cases of abuse, no systematic evidence exists that such practices are widespread. The effect of these laws will be to fragment healthcare and return medical services to the uncoordinated status that exists in the fee-for-service environment. If the purpose of legislation is to give patients freedom of choice, it could easily be accomplished by mandating that, if an employer offers health insurance to employees, an open-access product (such as an PPO) must be offered along with an HMO. Employees would, of course, have to pay the difference in price between these two types of plans.

A recent initiative by the health plans themselves also threatens this continuity of care and increases physicians' financial risk. This new type of product, called an open-access plan, functions like a capitated HMO, except that members can seek care from any plan physician without a referral from their primary care physicians (PCPs). These plans have several deleterious effects on the way services are delivered as well as on their costs. First, patients may see physicians not affiliated with their PCP's system of care. If they are hospitalized, the consultant may need to call another PCP to attend the patient, thus disrupting medically important continuity. Second, even if the patient is not hospitalized, communication between these two specialists may not be as efficient as under a regular working relationship. Third, many specialists have labored to develop good rapport with their PCP referral sources. Therefore, they stand to lose referrals in open-access plans. Fourth, because PCPs lose control of specialty referrals, their ability to be accountable for the cost and the quality of care is diminished. Finally, these arrangements violate one of the principles of insurance mentioned above—they provide more freedom of choice, but at no additional cost to the purchaser. Essentially, purchasers are getting a PPO at an HMO price. The additional cost of care resulting from this enhanced freedom is borne by the PCP and paid from capitation. This new product effectively converts the PCP into an indemnity insurer without an appropriate increase in compensation.

The third feature is the formerly voluntary nature of plan choice. In the past, workers whose employers provided health insurance had a chance to choose among several companies and types of products. Over the past several years, many employers have restricted this choice to one company and one or two products. This situation particularly applies to small employer groups. As a result of this singular choice and fierce competition among plans, in some markets HMOs have experienced as much as 25–40 percent membership turnover each year. The implication for physicians is that unless one belongs to a number of these plans and can retain one's patients, a severe loss in membership can suddenly occur.

An example is a pediatric practice in the Chicago area that lost 40 percent of its patients in one year because of their enrollment in health plans to which the group did not belong.

Finally, the cornerstone of HMOs is prepayment, particularly for physicians. Capitation, the practice of receiving a fixed amount in advance for provision of future services, fundamentally changes the way physicians view reimbursement. Under the fee-for-service system, the more one does, the more one is paid. Under capitation, one does not get paid more for doing more. Because capitation is a fixed sum and the volume of services the provider must provide are unknown, but estimable, this payment method makes the provider an insurer. It is therefore important for physicians to understand the services they are at risk for providing and to limit their potential liability by negotiating volume guarantees and by purchasing appropriate reinsurance (stop-loss coverage).

The major concern about a capitated system is, of course, the incentive to withhold necessary services. While there are certainly individual cases where that situation occurs, according to Berwick (1996), incentives for overutilization in the fee-for-service system are greater than those of underutilization with capitated plans.

Types of HMOs

Categorizing HMOs into different organizational types has been difficult because of the relatively fluid nature of contracting relationships among all types of healthcare providers. Despite these different typologies, it is useful to characterize these plans on the basis of their historical origins and to understand that newer forms are evolutionary modifications. The type of HMO plan can be defined by the relationship physicians have with the plan and by the organizational structure they create to contract to provide services. The first traditional type is the group or staff model. Under this type of plan, the HMO delivers services at one or more locations through a group of physicians. If the group is independent of the HMO but delivers care exclusively to its members, it is called a *group model.* The prototype is the Kaiser-Permanente Medical Group. When physicians are employees of the HMO, it is termed a *staff model.* In these models, physicians traditionally see only patients enrolled in that particular HMO. Recently, physicians in some of these plans have started to care for patients with other types of insurance.

The second traditional type of HMO is the individual practice association (IPA). In this type of organization, individual community physicians contract with one or more HMOs and see capitated patients in the same setting as their fee-for-service patients. Sometimes, HMOs will contract with individual physicians to form this type of plan. Increasingly,

HMOs contract with organizations that act as intermediaries between them and individual practitioners. Frequently, hospitals are helping physicians organize so they can access IPA contracts. This latter type of organization is the origin of the term *hospital-based IPA.*

A third form of HMO is the network model, which is a hybrid between a group model and an IPA. In this arrangement, independent multispecialty groups contract with one or more plans to deliver care to capitated members as well as fee-for-service patients.

The IPA and network models have been the fastest growing types of plans for at least two reasons. First, they give HMO members more freedom of choice than the group or staff model. As mentioned above, this feature is important to patients, and plans are pushing this benefit. Second, most HMOs are getting out of the "bricks and mortar" business—that is, they want to own less and contract out for more, particularly if they can shift financial risk to providers.

Financial Features of HMOs

While a full discussion of the financial features of HMOs is beyond the scope of this chapter, it is useful to look at the flow of funds in prepaid plans. Table 2.3 is an example of the distribution of premiums based on a capitated plan. Note that the percentages in this table are only approximate and depend on such features as what benefits are included in each category, reinsurance limits, and carve-outs (services for which the plan is entirely responsible). Often, these services are subcontracted to a third party that assumes full risk for caring for these patients.

Table 2.3 Distributing Prepaid Premiums

40% Physician Capitation	40% Hospital Fund	20% Administration
Physician fees 　Inpatient 　Outpatient 　Referrals	Inpatient hospital charges Surgicenter charges (Facility Only)	Operating costs Pharmaceuticals
Outpatient services 　Laboratory 　Radiology 　Therapies	Skilled nursing 　Facility 　Home Care	Reinsurance for 　special services 　Transplants 　Cardiac surgery 　Chronic hemodialysis
Stop-loss insurance	Durable equipment Stop-loss Insurance	Psychiatry/chemical 　dependency

Of the two sources of payment for physicians, the one receiving the most attention is capitation. While that portion is certainly important and constitutes the major monthly cash flow for physicians, an equally significant component is the hospital fund (sometimes called institutional service fund, medical incentive fund, or Part A fund). At the end of each contract year, physicians typically split the savings in this fund with the HMO. Because HMOs achieve their cost savings by reducing rates of unnecessary hospitalization (Miller and Luft 1993), this fund is their main source of plan profits. Likewise, profitability for physicians comes mostly from savings in this fund rather than from capitation. Therefore, physicians who understand capitated managed care are more likely to direct their utilization efforts to inpatient services rather than potentially withholding capitated services (Gabel 1997).

Medicare HMOs

Currently, about 15 percent of Medicare recipients are covered by HMOs, with growth estimated at 80,000 members per month. Plans are concentrated in a few urban centers. The Health Care Financing Administration (HCFA) pays HMOs at the 95th percentile of what it would have spent on an average enrollee according to that person's age, gender, county of residence, and whether he or she lives at home or in a long-term care facility. This method is called the average adjusted per capita cost (AAPCC). To encourage more HMO plan participation in rural areas and to reduce federal spending, HCFA is considering several nonmutually exclusive proposals: reduce AAPCC to the 90th percentile, set a minimum floor for rural AAPCC amounts while lowering urban rates, introduce competitive bidding for these federal contracts, do away with the AAPCC system, and base payment on historical utilization rather than averages. This latter method would counter controversial criticisms that HMOs enroll healthier Medicare members. Like their commercial counterparts, Medicare HMOs achieve their profits largely from savings in rates of discretionary hospitalizations (Miller and Luft 1993; Angus et al. 1996).

Future Trends and Recommendations

Four current trends will characterize health insurance in the near future. First, premium rates will stabilize or decline. In mature managed care markets, such as California, these rates have already decreased. Because health plans are charging less and desire to maintain or increase profits, less will be available to pay providers. Second, the public will continue to demand increased freedom of choice of providers. Contrary to the principles of insurance mentioned above, consumers will not be willing to pay more for this benefit and insurers will not be willing to charge more for this benefit. Third, private employers and, increasingly, public payors are demanding more accountability for the quality of care they purchase. They are, in effect, asking for *value* for their premium dollar. Finally, health plans are shifting more financial risk to providers without commensurate compensation; thus, providers are being asked to do more with fewer financial resources.

To cope with these changes, physicians and nonphysicians must work cooperatively to develop integrated systems of care. These systems do not have to be under a common ownership, but they must be coordinated to deliver efficient, high-quality services. Some changes necessary for physician-system integration to evolve are listed in Table 2.4.

Physicians have also successfully organized their own insurance plans. Some of these plans have even been sold to publicly traded insurers. Unfortunately, once sold, physicians find themselves to be employees subject to shrinking salaries and the same loss of control that prompted formation of their own company in the first place. Provider-sponsored plans are certainly feasible, but they must overcome the barriers listed in Table 2.5.

To overcome these barriers, physicians must educate themselves about the structure and function of managed care plans; continue the organizational trend to formation of medical groups; overcome inter-specialty cultural issues and work for common missions, goals, and objectives; secure adequate start-up and working capital, preferably from themselves and through their own borrowing power; invest heavily, but wisely, in information systems; and be willing to give up some personal control for the good of the group.

In 1762, Oliver Goldsmith wrote: "It is ... difficult to induce a number of free beings to cooperate for their mutual benefit" (Goldsmith

Table 2.4 Some Necessary Changes for Physician-System Integration

Current State	Desired State
Specialty focus	Primary care focus
Inpatient focus	Outpatient focus
Acute care model	Continuum of care model
Individual patient focus	Meeting needs of populations
Functional orientation	Process orientation
Short-term quality goals	Long-term assessments (Outcome-oriented)
Summary: A Cooperative Relationship	**An Integrated Clinical System**

Table 2.5 Organizational and Managerial Obstacles to Formation of Provider-Sponsored Plans

---

- Lack of education/experience regarding managed care and health systems
- Lack of appropriate organizational structure/relationships
- Lack of a functional, cohesive culture
- Inadequate capital
- Inadequate information systems
- Dysfunctional control issues

1970). If the medical profession and its nonclinical partners can put aside their differences, we can regain control of the healthcare system and implement changes in the best interests of the public we serve.

References

Angus, D., W. Linde-Zwirble, C. Sirio, A. Rotondi, L. Chelluri, R. Newbold, J. Lave, and M. Pinsky. 1996. "The Effect of Managed Care on ICU Length of Stay." *Journal of the American Medical Association* 276 (14): 1075–82.

Anonymous. 1988. "Insuring the Uninsured: Options and Analysis." Prepared by the Congressional Research Service. Washington, DC: Library of Congress, 11–40.

Berwick, D. 1996. "Payment by Capitation and the Quality of Care." *New England Journal of Medicine* 335 (16): 1227–31.

Friedman, E. 1995. "The Compromise and the Afterthought: Medicare and Medicaid after 30 Years." *Journal of the American Medical Association* 274 (3): 278–82.

Gabel, J. 1997. "Ten Ways HMOs Have Changed During the 1990s." *Health Affairs* 16 (3): 134–45.

Gold, M., M. Sparer, and K. Chu. 1996. "Medicaid Managed Care: Lessons From Five States." *Health Affairs* 15 (3): 153–66.

Goldsmith, O. 1970. *The Citizen of the World*. London, England: J.M. Dent and Sons, Ltd.

Hsiao, W., P. Braun, D. Dunn, E. Becker, M. DeNicola, and T. Ketcham. 1988. "Results and Policy Implications of the Resource-Based Relative Value Study." *New England Journal of Medicine* 319 (13): 881–88.

Iglehart, J. 1992. "The American Health Care System, Private Insurance." *New England Journal of Medicine* 326 (25): 1715–20.

Miller, R., and H. Luft. 1993. "Managed Care: Past Evidence and Potential Trends." *Frontiers of Health Services Management* 9 (3): 3–37.

Roe, B. 1981. "The UCR Boondoggle—A Death Knell for Private Practice?" *New England Journal of Medicine* 305 (1): 41–45.

Rowland, D., and K. Hanson. 1996. "Medicaid: Moving to Managed Care." *Health Affairs* 15 (3): 150–52.

Source Book of Health Insurance Data. 1996. Washington, DC: Health Insurance Association of America.

The Physician Executive: A Growing and Evolving Role

Deborah Shlian

W RITING ABOUT the growing and evolving role of the physician executive is as difficult as predicting future developments in our national healthcare delivery and financing system. Unprecedented and accelerated changes in the past 20 years have greatly modified the political and economic structure of American healthcare, and this has resulted in a new marketplace dynamic with medicine emerging as a trillion-dollar-a-year business. Whereas organizational efforts were originally focused on utilization review and establishing primary care–centered healthcare delivery systems, this new paradigm places greater emphasis on improving patient access and streamlining administrative burdens while still measuring outcomes.

Within this chaotic landscape, the emerging role of the physician executive is likewise in a state of flux. Where once the job description of an administrative physician leader was relatively straightforward, great diversity exists today in the scope of duties, responsibilities, and interactions with the business side of the organization. At the same time that there are more potential job options, there is often less long-term security. Given that, how should medical managers deal with this present level of uncertainty? How should they prepare themselves to take advantage of this brave new world?

Where We've Been

To answer such questions, one needs first to understand the evolution of the physician executive's role. Prior to the accelerated rise of managed care in the past two decades, most physicians had been office-based, solo, fee-for-service practitioners who managed their own offices and had little need for sophisticated business strategies or organizational skills. Leadership roles, other than those in professional organizations such as the American Medical Association or specialty societies, could be found only in academia or within hospitals. Academic physicians with seniority (generally those whose vitae included long lists of publications), became department chairs who juggled minor administrative responsibilities with teaching and research duties. A small number shed full-time clinical roles to become medical school deans. Generally, the only hospital-based physician leaders were department chiefs with part-time administrative functions. Like their academic counterparts, only a few of them assumed full-time management positions. Until World War II, far more doctors were hospital CEOs than there are today. After the war, a transition occurred, and nonphysicians entered the medical administration corps. Former military hospital managers were eager to do the same thing in the civilian world. At the same time, physicians were willing to relinquish whatever administrative roles they had because healthcare technology was advancing, and most preferred to devote their time to clinical practice.

For years, the few physician hospital administrators who did exist tended to be retired military men, disabled physicians, and even some unable to succeed in private practice. As administrators, they were generally shunted into clinically focused areas such as education, medical staff credentialing and hiring, and quality assurance oversight. Mainstream management, including financial and planning responsibilities, was handled by nonphysician professional administrators who had graduated from hospital administration programs. The same was true of doctors at the helm of the various group practices around the country. These jobs were a thankless hardship, with no extra pay to manage a group of peers who had the same status as their leader. Many group practices simply required each doctor member to preside as titular head for a year. Consequently, no one really learned how to lead, and the top physician had virtually no authority. With relatively little competition in the marketplace, groups thrived in this period, despite a lack of sophisticated medical management.

However, the spectacular growth of managed care in the past two decades has changed the situation. Healthcare organizations are becoming larger and increasingly complex, particularly as smaller independent practices merge into larger integrated entities or become part of huge national organizations. This, combined with the need for greater effectiveness and productivity, has created opportunities for physician executives. No longer becoming managers by default, most now see administration as a full-time career and are strategically planning and implementing the transition from clinician to executive. Increasingly, too, these individuals choose to leave clinical practice entirely, bringing into play new sets of dynamics with their clinician peers as well as with nonphysician executives.

Data

While there are no good statistics on the exact number of physician managers in the United States, about 12,209 physicians reported "administration" as their primary professional activity in the American Medical Association's Physician Masterfile in 1980. In 1985, the total number rose to 13,810 and in 1995 it rose again to 16,345 (*Physician Characteristics and Distribution in the U.S., 1996–1997*). A sample of 878 of the 1985 group was interviewed by telephone by the Wisconsin Survey Research Laboratory (Kindig and Lastri-Quros 1986). The average physician executive interviewed was found to be a white male, 54 years old, with 7 years in a current position requiring 65 percent administrative time and 20 percent patient care time (see Table 3.1). Thirty percent worked in hospitals, 47 percent in either government or educational organizations, 5 percent in HMOs, 5 percent in healthcare corporations, and 4 percent in industry.

Most respondents in the 1985 survey acknowledged that moving into administration was an afterthought, a reactive response to an opportunity. As a group, they generally did not seek their management roles, and virtually all still retained clinical responsibilities, seeing patients at least 20 percent of the time. Their administrative duties were primarily focused on personnel management—supervising other physicians and professional staff, medical education, and quality assurance. Their biggest problems were communicating with and disciplining physicians and keeping administration from interfering with the physicians in their clinical work.

A 1997 telephone survey of 1,539 physician executives conducted by Shlian and Associates, Inc., produced several results that suggest some significant changes in the past decade (see Table 3.2). First, the average age of the group was 48, a full six years younger than the average individual in the Wisconsin survey. Second, although the 1985 survey did not report respondents' specialties, we believe that many more physician administrators came from surgical and non–primary care specialties, such

Table 3.1 Characteristics of Physician Executives, 1985

Characteristic	Response
Average age	54.2 years
Average years in administration	18.6 years
Average number of previous administrative positions	2.3 positions
Average years in current administrative position	7.2 years
Average number of hours worked	54.2 hours per week
Percentage of time in administration	64.9%
Percentage of time in patient care	20.5%
Mean total annual income	$110,300
Type of organization	
Hospital	30%
Educational institute	24%
Government agency	23%
Group practice/HMO	5%
Healthcare corporation	5%
Industry	4%
Other	8%

Source: Responses to a telephone survey from 878 physicians whose self-reported primary professional activity was administration in the 1986 American Medical Association's Physician Masterfile.

Table 3.2 Characteristics of Physician Executives, 1997

Characteristic	Response
Average age	48 years
Average years in administration	8 years
Average number of previous administrative positions	3 positions
Average years in current administrative position	1.5 years
Average number of hours worked	50 hours per week
Percentage of time in administration (only 66 practiced any clinical medicine)	100%

Source: Shlian and Associates, Inc.

as OB-GYN or psychiatry, than is true today. Our survey found that most (74 percent) were board certified in three primary care specialties: internal medicine, family medicine, and pediatrics (see Table 3.3). Recent articles by other recruiters confirm the fact that companies today overwhelmingly favor primary care physicians for executive positions (Lyons and Cejka 1994).

A third difference in our survey was the type of organizations in which physician executives worked. Most of the current group were

Table 3.3 Physician Executives by Specialty

Specialty (Board Certified)	Number	Percentage
Internal medicine	671	44%
Family medicine	304	20
Pediatrics	160	10
Psychiatry	72	5
OB-GYN	70	5
Emergency medicine	60	4
Surgery	45	3
Preventive medicine	33	2
Anesthesiology	22	1
Radiology	12	1
ENT	12	1
Neurology	10	1
Urology	8	1
Pathology	8	1
Ophthalmology	8	1
Orthopedics	6	0
Dermatology	4	0
Allergy	4	0
Rehabilitation medicine	1	0
No boards	29	2
Total	1,539	

Source: Shlian and Associates, Inc.

employed in managed healthcare organizations, including group- or staff-model HMOs; health plans; MSOs; integrated health systems; review companies; and carve-outs or insurance companies (70.3 percent), as opposed to hospitals (9.7 percent), academia (4.9 percent), and government agencies (2.7 percent) (see Table 3.4).

A fourth difference can be seen in the fact that, on average, the current group surveyed already had had an average of three previous administrative jobs, reflecting the greater level of turnover of positions in the past decade.

A fifth difference was the average number of years of clinical medicine practiced before making the switch to administration (8 years for the 1997 group versus 20 years in earlier studies). The average number of years in the current administrative job was 1.5 years for the 1997 group versus 7.2 for the 1985 respondents. Moreover, only 66 of the 1997 group (4.3 percent) still performed any clinical work; the majority were full-time administrators.

A sixth difference was related to gender. According to AMA statistics, only 9.6 percent (1,178) of all physician administrators were women

Table 3.4 Organizations in Which Physician Executives Work

Type of Organization	Number	Percentage
Hospital	150	9.70%
Academia	76	4.90
Government agency	41	2.70
Consulting firm	49	3.20
Industry/Pharmaceutical	34	2.20
Managed care		
Insurance company	306	20
Health plans	275	18
Group/HMO	323	21
MSO	60	4
Integrated health systems	35	2.30
Carve-outs	17	1.10
Review companies	61	4
Other	112	7.30

Source: Shlian and Associates, Inc., telephone survey of 1,539 physician executives.

in 1980. This number had risen to 14.7 percent (2,399) by 1995. In our group, 20.1 percent of the physician executives were women, more than double the total number and percentage in fifteen years (see Table 3.5).

Finally, of the group surveyed in 1985, only 3 percent held graduate management degrees other than an M.P.H. (held by 9.9 percent). Yet 84 percent felt that management degrees were advisable. In 1995, Witt/Kieffer, Ford, Hadelman, and Lloyd surveyed physicians in management positions (Anonymous 1995) and found that 9 percent had M.B.A.'s, up from 6 percent in 1990 and from none at all in 1979. Another 35 percent in this survey stated that they intended to pursue an M.B.A. or were already working on one. In our 1997 survey, 21 percent (322) had some graduate management degree: 12 percent (188) had M.B.A.'s, 6 percent (93) had M.P.H.'s, 0.5 percent (7) had M.P.A.'s, and 0.5 percent (7) had M.H.A.'s (see Table 3.6).

Table 3.5 Male versus Female Physician Executives

	1980	1985	1995
Males	11,031	12,326	13,946
Females	1,178	1,484	2,399
Total in administration	12,209	13,810	16,345
Total physicians	467,679	552,716	720,325

Source: Physician Characteristics and Distribution in the U.S., 1996/97 Edition Chicago, Ill.: American Medical Association, 1997.

Table 3.6 Graduate Degrees Held by Physician Executives

Graduate Degrees	Number	Percentage
M.B.A.	188	12%
M.P.H.	93	6
M.P.A.	7	0.50
M.H.A.	7	0.50
M.S.	5	0.30
Ph.D.	8	0.50
J.D.	14	0.90
Total	322	21

Source: Shlian and Associates, Inc.

All of these differences demonstrate that today's physician executives have a profile different from that of their predecessors; they are making the decision to move into administration earlier in their careers—and that decision is proactive. Many seek to meld medical and business acumen by obtaining additional professional management training and credentials. In fact, a large percentage (92 percent in our survey) now feel that an M.B.A. or other management degree is a requirement for entry into a full-time management career.

Respondents in the 1997 survey stated that they had opted for their management positions as "part of their overall career enhancement." Most said that their interest in management grew out of a desire to be a policymaker, offering a chance to provide top management support for medical practitioners and to influence the larger picture—how groups of patients received care and the environment in which services are delivered. Many also noted the emerging importance of professional roles in managing the technical complexity of cost containment. A few stated that their career transitions arose, at least partially, out of "frustration with what's happening in medicine today" because of loss of professional autonomy and of changes in the doctor-patient relationship. All felt that, in addition to the well-trained, broadly based primary care physician who is currently at the core of the healthcare delivery system, the skilled physician executive acts as a liaison and facilitator among all constituencies: patients, healthcare providers, managed care organizations, large employer groups, government policymakers, and hospitals.

Increase in Scope of Responsibilities

Concomitant with the dramatic increase in total numbers of physician managers today has been the growth in the breadth of responsibilities taken on by these individuals. In reviewing several dozen job descriptions and information obtained through our survey, it became clear that no matter what their titles—medical director, vice president of medical affairs, chief medical officer, or even CEO—physician managers are generally still considered the "medical leaders" of their organizations. Their responsibilities tend to focus on several key areas:

- **Utilization management** (UM)—Duties include guiding clinical policy, chairing UM committees, setting procedures, acting as liaison between providers and the organization—i.e., plan, group, or hospital—influencing behaviors of delegated groups, providing educational resources for professional staff and clinical decision makers, and analyzing UM reports and physician profiles.

- **Quality improvement**—Credentialing duties including peer review, leadership in accreditation process, chairing QA/peer review committees.

- **Grievance and appeals**—Including overseeing the clinical side of risk management as opposed to the legal and financial side—that is, providing leadership with respect to clinical complaints, identifying potential risk situations, implementing steps to minimize risk.

- **Network management/Provider relations**—Including overseeing physician relations, network recruitment/expansion efforts, and contract negotiations; and **Internal consultant**, providing clinical expertise to provider services within the organization, government relations and compliance, underwriting, and senior management in general.

The physicians in our survey with formal management training stated that they were able to use knowledge obtained in their training programs to enhance the performance of their duties—specifically, decision analysis, outcomes measures, operations research techniques, production models, and informatics (what Weil [1997] calls "clinical-fiscal performance methodological"). However, many were equally disappointed that they were not able to use their new skills in areas directly related to strategy, policy, and financial issues at the highest level of the organization (such as the board of directors). Physician executives have affected the formulation of standards and procedures and clinical protocols, but, for the most part, most have encountered barriers to moving into senior executive positions in which they could actually change the system at a macro level. Of the 1,539 individuals surveyed, only 24 were CEOs, and the majority of that group were heads of either entrepreneurial organizations (8) or group-model HMOs (6) (see Table 3.7). None were CFOs or COOs.

Is the disconnect expressed by these respondents true? That is, as physicians become more experienced in management and even obtain

Table 3.7 Titles Held by Physician Executives

Title	Number
Vice President of Medical Affairs	94
Chief Medical Officer	40
Medical Director	734
Associate Medical Director	334
Senior Medical Director	80
Chief Executive Officer*	24
Other	233

*Eight entrepreneurial firms, six group-model HMOs, three hospitals, one insurance company, one MSO, one university, two health plans, one PHO, one carve-out.
Source: Shlian and Associates, Inc.

professional management training, are they being excluded from the inner circle of senior executive positions? If this is the case, what is limiting career advancement? Is there any rationale for physician executives to be excluded as a class from these roles?

A recent article discussed this dilemma, citing a glass ceiling that seems to be preventing physician executives from achieving positions of top leadership and governance within healthcare organizations. According to Lazarus (1997), among several factors accounting for this phenomenon are a lack of formal training in administration, lack of mentoring either by other business-trained physicians in executive positions or by nonphysician senior executives, cultural differences between physicians and nonmedical healthcare executives, personality differences, and lack of administrative experience.

As mentioned, lack of formal training in administration is being remedied as an ever-increasing number of physicians obtain graduate business degrees. Lack of mentoring, on the other hand, is clearly an issue that needs to be addressed. Only a handful of middle manager respondents in the 1997 survey reported having senior managers in their organizations offer career guidance. Similarly, when asked if they had identified less experienced physician managers to sponsor and support in their career advancement, the answer was a resounding "no." As Lazarus points out, although the value of mentoring for business executives is unquestionable, physician executives have not learned that it should be the cornerstone of any human resource development plan. To compound the problem, many companies wrongly assume that, because they were mentored through clinical training, doctors do not need mentoring in their management roles. As a result, physician executives may need to seek mentors outside of their organizations, perhaps in business school alumni groups or professional groups such as the American College of Physician Executives. Moreover, because there are still so relatively few physician leaders at the highest levels, it may mean finding nonphysician mentors.

On the other hand, it may perpetuate a stereotype to justify the glass ceiling on the basis that medical education has traditionally socialized physicians to focus on the needs of individual patients; to make quick, scientifically based, reasoned decisions; to think more short term; to be more reactive than proactive; and to work independently. In the fee-for-service world, most physicians were able to run extraordinarily successful businesses, generating 30 to 40 percent of gross revenues for end-of-the-year take-home pay—a feat very few American businesses could match (Mack 1997). The move from "street corner" entrepreneurial medicine to corporate delivery system, however, requires a change in approach and skills for success. Many clinical curricula are beginning to teach the value of working as a member of a healthcare team, emphasizing epidemiology and preventive medicine by focusing on "big-picture areas," such as population-based outcomes measures, disease management, quality of life, and other long-term qualitative issues. Students are taught to weigh various factors involved in a decision to put into perspective the relationship between cost and the impact of a decision on a patient's health. These skills, required to be a good clinician today, are directly transferable to the role of manager. Above and beyond the fact that the socialization of physicians within medical school is changing, many doctors who aspire to executive roles are entering graduate schools of business administration where they are socialized alongside nonphysician executives and younger graduate students.

Likewise, the notion that those with personality types specifically attracted to medicine are less likely to be successful as managers should be challenged (Lazarus 1997). Neither medical schools nor graduate schools perform personality tests on applicants to their programs. Consequently, there is likely to be a mix of personality types among individuals of both professions. O'Connor and Shewchuk (1993) apparently did not study physician executives as a group but simply compared practicing physicians to nonphysician healthcare executives. When one of our clients recently used the Myers-Briggs Type Indicator as part of its hiring process, the results were mixed, with most of the physicians demonstrating what the authors claim to be the quintessential business type personalities (extrovert, sensing, thinking, and judging). Perhaps ironically, several of the nonphysician candidates had "physician" personalities (introversion, intuition, thinking, and judging). Lazarus (1997) makes the point that, notwithstanding this "personality type" thesis, leadership and vision are independent of personality anyway.

Given evidence that a glass ceiling does exist, much of the rationale provided is less than convincing. When asked how they could explain the barriers to senior positions, many of the respondents in our 1997 survey stated that they believed the problem to be entirely a "turf" issue: "Nonphysician executives," some respondents claimed, "feel threatened by someone with a management degree that might very well be from the same business school as that of the CEO or the COO *and* a medical degree; they don't want to invite doctors into the inner circle for fear they will take over." Interestingly, a physician who is a senior consultant with a very prestigious national firm confided that, when submitting proposals to clients for high-level strategic issues, he often omits his M.D. title, emphasizing instead his financial and general management expertise. "Senior management in particular does not seem to appreciate the value a physician can bring to the team as a unique professional. In fact, when a strategic assessment is completed, invariably the members selected by the client to represent the company on the implementation team are the CEO, CFO, COO, and marketing. Rarely, member services are included and *never* medical directors—even at the corporate level. This is unfortunate, because not only is it demoralizing, but their potential input is lost." Many respondents felt that bias existed even against physicians who demonstrated good business skills.

Today, a greater wedge may be being driven between physician and nonphysician administrators simply because the market for managers in general appears to have weakened. A recent article in the *National Business Employment Weekly* cited a new phenomenon of layoffs of the most senior level managers, creating a glut of candidates in a consolidated market (Solomon 1997). It is not surprising, then, that administrators would resent physicians "horning in on their territory." To compete for scarce positions paying annual base salaries of $150,000 and up, managers must have impressive leadership and marketing skills. Nonphysician administrators often have spent 10 to 20 years making very low salaries relative to physicians, moving up through the ranks from areas such as underwriting, contracting, sales, and marketing. For physician managers, the catch-22 is that many who seek senior-level opportunities are not afforded the same kind of exposure to these key areas as are their nonphysician counterparts.

In 1992, Kindig wrote: "The importance of the physician executive will continue to grow. Many future physician executives will hold modern master's degrees in health management; most will fill boundary-spanning roles emphasizing clinical management science. Some will successfully compete for CEO positions. The emergence of a stronger role for physician executives will require change in the structure of the management team, but healthcare organizations that are able to make the necessary adjustments will be rewarded with better performance in both cost control and quality improvement" (Kindig and Kovner 1992).

Those words were prophetic. Six years since its writing, data show that the number of physicians in management has grown, that more and more physician executives are obtaining management degrees, and that most physician executives are in full-time medical director roles that offer opportunities to affect healthcare in important ways. There is, however, need for further movement at the senior operations level. As Kindig suggests, this will require a change in the structure of the healthcare team. To accomplish such change, however, will likely take time. A major reason more physician executives have not reached "senior leadership" positions is that the current principal competitive strategy within the healthcare industry is based on consolidation and consequent increased marketshare (i.e., greater patient base). There is, therefore, relatively little emphasis on quality versus cost. As a result, the insight and expertise that only a physician manager can theoretically bring to an organization has not been seen as particularly valuable.

In a recent editorial in the *Journal of the American Medical Association*, economist Victor Fuchs (1997) stated that while managed care has performed a useful social function in reducing unnecessary services, "the big unknown is whether further large gains are possible once the gross weaknesses have been eliminated." Well-trained, experienced physician executives are logically in the best position to identify further areas of cost reduction while still maintaining high-quality care. At this critical juncture in the evolution of American medicine, physician executives in senior leadership can bring a credibility to healthcare that neither nonphysician managers nor physicians without management training can provide.

What about the Future?

A number of trends are listed below that, for the near future, will likely create more and new opportunities at all levels for medical managers as organizational and role restructuring continues.

Continued Growth of Managed Care

Recent trends indicate further increases in commercial, Medicare, and Medicaid enrollment in managed care (more than 58 million by the end of 1995). As more people move into managed care, an intense education effort of providers, enrollees, and employer groups becomes critical. Members with special needs will create opportunities in such disparate areas as home health and genetic counseling. According to the *Wall Street Journal*, in the 1990s home health care spending has soared 30 percent a year, with $16 billion spent in 1995 (Anders 1997).

On the physician side, the managed care trend, especially in more mature markets, has turned many physician practices inside out. Managed care organizations' reliance on primary care and the current emphasis on the gatekeeper model have reversed the preferred ratio of primary care physicians to specialists. At the same time, companies such as Blue Shield Plans and United Healthcare are considering alternatives through the so-called "open access" model. Carve-outs are being developed in such areas as oncology, cardiology, and mental health, allowing specialists direct access to patients with high-cost acute or chronic illness. These changes all create a greater need for sophisticated information systems to manage patient flow, to assess effectiveness of treatment, to conduct physician profiling, and to monitor medical case management initiatives. Physician executives interested in these areas may find more opportunities in such newly created roles as director of disease management, director of medical informatics, and director of clinical effectiveness.

Consolidation of the Marketplace

Currently there is a trend to capitalizing managed care operations and to spreading risk. Capitation contracts have caused organizations to "need to grow" and to grow rapidly. This has spurred a rush of mergers among HMOs and other managed care companies, particularly in markets that are vertically integrated or those with an excess of specialists and hospitals. Mergers are also occurring among and between hospitals, insurers, and physician groups. Large academic medical centers are merging with healthcare delivery systems. Physician groups are forming alliances with hospitals. Local HMOs are merging with one another or are being acquired by large insurers (e.g., United Healthcare and MetraComp, U.S. Healthcare and Aetna).

Paradoxically, dozens of new HMOs sprang up in 1996 at the same time that existing HMOs consolidated. The total number of HMOs jumped from about 550 in 1993 to about 630 in 1996, according to InterStudy (Jacob 1997), including about 60 new HMOs formed last year. Many of the new HMOs are local, physician-owned plans. Provider-run plans are especially popular in states such as Georgia, which recently passed insurance regulation favorable to their formation. Of the dozen or so HMOs that applied for licenses in Georgia last year, about half were physician-owned.

The future of these upstart HMOs, given unstable market dynamics, is in question. An InterStudy survey of 126 HMOs established in 1985 found that, within seven years, half were bought out by other plans. So it is conceivable that, as HMOs pursue economies of scale and market clout through mergers and acquisitions, small HMOs will become targets for larger companies. It is predicted that many physician-owned plans will not be able to survive against large, well-capitalized insurers, However, the future of HMOs in markets where large provider groups have directly contracted with a consortium of employers is another interesting question to be answered.

Nevertheless, health professionals will be taking a much more active role in managed care. According to an industry consultant, all groups of physicians who have succeeded in the long term both qualitatively and operationally have involved physician-led, physician-driven change. "Regimes that are externally imposed and most often anchored in purely economic assumptions will not bear the fullest fruit and could even backfire" (Gerber and Bojlefeld 1997).

Marketshare as a Competitive Advantage

For insurers, marketshare, not profit, will be the driving force in 1997, pushing out competitors by increasing enrollment. In markets where competition is heated, such as California, profit margins will be very low—from 2 to 3 percent, perhaps as low as a half percent. One reason is that HMOs are in the last year of three- or four-year contracts with companies for employee health coverage. They made huge profits the first year but little the third year. That may be acceptable for insurers with enough capital to hold onto marketshare, but it means that others will fold or sell. Generally, one of the first signs is downsizing of personnel, especially middle management. Given this trend, it is important for physician executives to do careful market analyses as well as look closely at an individual company before signing on or even staying on.

Increasing Employer Clout

When negotiating new contracts with employer groups in the next few years, insurers will have to maintain low premium prices, because employers and consumers will no longer tolerate huge boosts. Analysts predict an overall increase in premiums of between 3 and 4 percent with premiums for HMOs to rise 2 to 4 percent and for PPOs 7 percent, while indemnity premiums will jump as much as 10 percent. At the same time insurers are having a difficult time negotiating advantageous contract terms, with hospitals and physician groups regaining bargaining clout by merging into larger, stronger entities and becoming more savvy negotiators. This trend has enabled physician executives with contract negotiation skills to participate in an area heretofore off-limits to them, as at least some insurers understand the value of someone who can speak to the providers in their language and at the same time appreciate business issues.

Increased Consumer Voice

Continuing a trend felt in 1996, consumers will become more vocal and assertive about the quality of their plans. As managed care becomes the norm, consumers will push for quality safeguards, flexibility to seek care outside the network, and full disclosure of plan restrictions. While some observers consider legislative solutions such as mandatory 48-hour hospitalization following childbirth a fad, consumers (both individually and through large public interest groups such as AARP) have spoken, and healthcare organizations that want to stay in business are heeding the message that the managed care industry is going to be under close scrutiny. This is compounded by the fact that many employer groups are considering increasing employee contributions to their health benefits. As the public is given more responsibility for healthcare purchasing decisions, there is more incentive to understand what they are buying. This trend has produced a growing number of quality measures, or at least proxies for quality, such as NCQA's HEDIS and patient satisfaction surveys. Physician executives with interests and training in epidemiology and preventive medicine (generally with M.P.H. degrees) are increasingly finding new job opportunities with insurers, provider groups, consulting firms, employer groups, and research institutions as a result of this trend.

Next-Stage Cost Reductions

Of course, pleasing the customer does not imply that insurers can ignore costs. There has been significant progress in cost reduction, but much of it has been "low-hanging fruit," such as reducing hospital stays. The next stage is going to involve more substantive changes as to how healthcare is delivered. Integrated health information systems, aggressive disease management programs, and outcomes measures are all seen as strategies to reduce costs and thus as opportunities for medical managers—particularly those with specialized technical skills and training.

Employer-Based Insurance Will Likely Continue

For the next several years, employer-based insurance will continue to be the mechanism through which Americans obtain health insurance. But as more people become self-employed and act as independent contractors, there may be increased demand for widespread reforms in how healthcare coverage is purchased and administered. If health insurance purchasing cooperatives, such as those in Florida, gain popularity, provider-owned groups may benefit, because employers will simply give employees vouchers to purchase health insurance plans. That simple step would eliminate the key barrier to the entry of new plans. It would enable even small employers to offer hundreds of HMOs in given markets and pave the way for numerous provider-sponsored health plans. If the economics are compelling enough, it would likely be attractive to employers, two in five of whom today no longer want to pay more than half their workers' health insurance costs (Anonymous 1997). All these new provider-owned plans will need physician leaders.

Bottom Line

The rate of change sweeping America's healthcare delivery system has obviously accelerated. In this new environment, leadership roles for physician executives are much more varied and often more focused in specific "specialty areas" (e.g., quality management, medical informatics, disease management) than even a few years ago. Despite the growth in opportunities in many different kinds of healthcare organizations, the question still looms as to whether in the future more physician executives with broad-based leadership and organization skills will be able to move into the highest business executive levels. At the same time, there is far less job security in organizations today than ever before.

How should medical managers deal with this new level of uncertainty? First, acknowledge it. Second, if deciding to be part of it, study emerging trends and target opportunities compatible with personal skills, training, and interests. Finally, be prepared—emotionally as well as financially—to take a certain level of risk and go for it. Defining roles, organizational dynamics, and credentials for physician executives is still a nascent concept. It is clear, however, that physician executives will need to be leaders rather than followers if healthcare delivery is to move in a more positive direction in the future.

References

Anders, G. 1997. "Home Health Care," *Wall Street Journal*, Section II, March 6.

Anonymous. 1995. "The Second Degree: MDs with MBAs." *Southern California Medicine* (January): 17.

Anonymous. 1997. "The Trend in Business: Pass the Expense Back to Workers." *Medical Economics* 74 (5): 53.

Fuchs, V. 1997. "Managed Care and Merger Mania." *Journal of the American Medical Association* 277 (11): 920–21.

Gerber, P., and M. Bojlefeld. 1997. "What's Ahead for Managed Care in 1997: The Shape of Medical Care Hangs in the Balance." *Physician's Management* 37 (1): 36–47.

Jacob, J. 1997. "Local Health Plans Could Top Big HMOs." *American Medical News* 40 (3): 3, 28, 31.

Kindig, D., and A. Kovner. 1992. *The Role of the Physician Executive: Cases and Commentary*. Chicago: Health Administration Press.

Kindig, D., and S. Lastri-Quros. 1986. "Administrative Medicine: A New Specialty?" *Health Affairs* 5 (4): 146–56.

Lazarus, A. 1997. "Breaking the Glass Ceiling." *Physician Executive* 23 (3): 8–13.

Lyons, M., and S. Cejka. 1994. "Getting a Firm Grip on the Realities for Physician Executives." *Physician Executive* 20 (6): 8–12.

Mack, K. 1997. "Surviving in Style in a Changing Business Environment." *American Medical News* 40 (12): 32.

O'Connor, S., and R. Shewchuk. 1993. "Enhancing Administrator-Clinician Relationships: The Role of Psychological Type." *Healthcare Management Review* 18 (2): 57–65.

Physician Characteristics and Distribution in the U.S., 1996–1997. 1997. Chicago: American Medical Association.

Solomon, G. 1997. "Demand Weakens for HMO Executives." *National Business Employment Weekly* (September 22): 35–36.

Weil, T. 1997. "Which Degree Should You Choose?" *Physician Executive* 23 (3): 4–7.

Physician Executive Development and Education

Jay Noren and David A. Kindig

T HE ROLE of the physician executive in the American health-care system is evolving at a rapid and accelerating rate. Although physicians have always served as technical leaders, the executive role only recently, initially in the 1970s, began to emerge as a new medical discipline. Its rise parallels the maturation of the American healthcare industry from cottage industry 50 years ago to the modern corporate enterprise. The corporate character of healthcare reflects the industry's prominence in the national economy. Current expenditures are $1 trillion and 14 percent of gross national product (GNP), compared to $69 billion and 7.2 percent of GNP in 1970 and a pale $2.5 billion in 1935 (Lee and Estes 1997; Starr 1982). The increasing need for and complexity of the physician executive role also mirrors the growth in healthcare organizational complexity from predominantly solo practice and indemnity insurance 50 years ago to today's group practice, prepaid healthcare, managed care, and both horizontal and vertical integration comprising hospitals, physician groups, and financing mechanisms.

Trends in the Physician Executive Role

Since the new physician executive role emerged two decades ago, its character has changed in four principal dimensions:
- numbers of physician executives;
- time commitment and management level;

- clinical activity; and
- educational background

First, the numbers of physicians with primary management roles has virtually exploded in the past two decades. An analysis of both full- and part-time physicians in management reveals a 38 percent increase between 1977 and 1986 to an estimated 27,635 full-time equivalent physicians. Similarly, membership in the American College of Physician Executives during its 20-year history has grown dramatically, from 64 in 1975 to 2,000 in 1985, and then a six-fold growth to more than 12,000 in 1995. The 1994 American Medical Association physician database revealed 15,684 physicians in such roles (2.52 percent of all physicians) (LeTourneau and Curry 1997; Kindig 1997).

Second, an increasing proportion of physician executives serve in full-time management roles. Two decades ago, typical physician executives served in part-time leadership roles in hospitals and group practices, with titles such as president of the medical staff, department chair, vice president for medical affairs, chief of staff, director of medical education, president of the board of directors, and director of quality assurance, among others. Although several similar part-time positions continue as important leadership functions, vice president for medical affairs, medical director, and other positions have increasingly become full time. Development of more complex delivery structures in managed care organizations and integrated delivery systems has demanded these full-time roles. Consistent with movement toward more full-time commitment, physician executives now assume more senior line- and staff-management positions.

Third, the aforementioned trends diminish the feasibility of continued clinical practice for senior physician executives. When the role emerged two decades ago, virtually all physician executives maintained clinical practices—practices often substantial. Recently, the clinical role has changed significantly. LeTourneau and Curry's (1997) analysis notes " . . . the full-time physician executive who does not have a clinical practice is a relatively new phenomenon. Prior to the 1980s, most physician managers maintained at least a token clinical practice as they went about their management duties. [Today] physician executives have found it very difficult to maintain a clinical practice and adequately perform their management duties."

Fourth, physician executives' need for increasingly sophisticated management expertise has precipitated the drive toward formal graduate education. The number of graduate executive training programs for physicians has increased rapidly during the 1990s, as has the proportion of physician executives with management graduate degrees. A survey by the Physician Executive Management Center reported in 1993 that 31 percent of vice presidents for medical affairs have or are working on a management degree—a fact particularly noteworthy given that two decades ago that position often required only a part-time commitment (Sherer 1993).

Critical Talents, Skills, and Knowledge for Career Physician Executives

The critical ingredients of the successful physician executive group logically into three interrelated categories: integrative and adaptive talents, acquired skills and knowledge, and professional experience.

Integrative and Adaptive Talents

Integrative and adaptive talents, because they tend to be more subjective and less easily defined, elude analysis, evaluation, and measurement more than the other two categories. They are, nonetheless, critically important to physician executive competence. They derive substantially from personality traits and individual character developed throughout one's life experience. Although education may facilitate their development, traditional educational methods rarely suffice. Acquisition of these integrative and adaptive talents grows more from life experience than from formal education. A list of these ingredients is inevitably incomplete, but several are clearly most critical. Interpersonal effectiveness is the most important of the integrative and adaptive talents. Additional key competencies are diplomacy, sincerity, patience, objective listening, motivation of self and others, capacity for teamwork, and honesty.

Several of these ingredients hold particular relevance in the transition from clinical physician to physician executive. Personality traits and style differences reflected in clinical thinking versus management thinking underscore the personal challenge physicians face in this transition. Several of the integrative and adaptive ingredients differ in importance for the clinician compared to the manager. For example, team-building capacity and listening effectiveness correspond more to the manager's tendency for delegation, collaboration, and participative behaviors. Preference for quick decisiveness and direct action typifies the clinician, whereas the manager more readily tolerates decision processes in conditions of uncertainty, a planning role, and delayed gratification. While these contrasts are somewhat simplistic and artificial, they nonetheless illustrate the differences in style, in approaches to problems, and in adaptive techniques between clinicians and managers that complicate this personal transition.

LeTourneau and Curry (1997) note, "It is often stated by physician executives that their most difficult tasks are convincing physician colleagues that they are still physicians and convincing nonphysician management colleagues that they deserve to be viewed seriously as managers."

Kurtz (1994) described the contrast between the clinician and the manager in eight descriptors:

Clinician (physician)	Manager (physician executive)
Doer	Planner/designer
Reactive	Proactive
Inclined to immediate gratification	Accepting of delayed gratification
Decider	Delegator
Autonomy	Collaboration
Independent	Participative
Patient advocate	Organization advocate
Professional identification	Organization identification

Acquired Critical Skills and Knowledge

The knowledge and skill sets essential for physician executives overlap substantially with those of general management training typically found in business school M.B.A. programs. However, the differences exceed the similarities. Even traditional disciplines, such as finance, organizational behavior, and accounting, must, out of necessity, emphasize the unique elements of the healthcare industry.

The following knowledge and skill sets provide a comprehensive array divided into two groups: traditional management emphases and unique health industry emphases.

Traditional Management Emphases:
- Finance
- Organizational behavior
- Human resource management/personnel management
- Negotiation
- Communication (oral and written)
- Conflict resolution
- Applied decision making
- Management information systems and information technology
- Accounting
- Government relations
- Time management

Unique Health Industry Emphases:
- Healthcare professional staff management: recruitment, selection, retention

Physicians
Nurses
Other clinical specialties
Medical legal staff
Healthcare marketing
Healthcare public relations
Epidemiology
Medical record information systems
Use and analysis of large population health databases
Healthcare market analysis
Healthcare cost benefit/cost effectiveness analysis
Technology assessment
Healthcare quality improvement/quality assurance
Medical staff relations
Credentialing of clinicians
Evaluation of practice patterns for efficiency

Given the increasing breadth and depth of the physician executive role, it is difficult to reach consensus on the most important among these knowledge and skill sets. Dunham and Kindig's survey of 154 physician executives and 176 nonphysician healthcare executives resulted in condensation of top priority skills into four broad sets:

1. relations with medical staff;
2. quality assurance;
3. evaluation of practice pattern efficiency; and
4. definition of organizational goals, priorities, and directions. (Dunham, Kindig, and Schultz 1994)

Linney and Linney (1992) developed a longer list of top priority skills and knowledge, further modified by LeTourneau and Curry (1997), that expands on the four key skills sets of Dunham and Kindig. Amalgamation of these more detailed skills sets under the four Dunham-Kindig key groups provides a comprehensive and focused description of the essential elements necessary for the competent physician executive.

Relations with Medical Staff
Recruit physicians
Manage impaired physicians
Serve as liaison between administration and medical staff
Oversee credentialing and privileging of physicians
Develop provider relations
Resolve grievances, professional disputes, and
  interdepartmental problems
Coordinate interorganizational medical affairs

Consult among units on medical management issues

Develop and manage provider networks

Quality Assurance

Direct utilization review

Oversee medical quality management

Develop and manage overall medical quality systems and
procedures

Evaluation of Practice Pattern Efficiency

Evaluate physician performance

Manage physician performance

Oversee medical information systems

Definition of Organizational Goals, Priorities, and Directions

Serve on board of directors

Develop staffing plans

Prepare expense budget for medical department

Ensure compliance with mission statement, appropriate
policies, and bylaws

Participate in strategic planning

Develop medical marketing plans

Manage and coordinate contractual relationships

Clearly, several of these specific skill sets could apply to more than
one of the four Dunham-Kindig groupings. Nonetheless, this array provides a framework for thinking about high-priority skills and knowledge
for the physician executive.

Experiential Preparation for the Physician Executive

The diversity and complexity of organizations, people, and professions
to which the physician executive must effectively relate makes extensive
and broad experiential preparation essential. High-quality management
education and personality and character traits facilitating integrative
and adaptive talents are essential but not sufficient for the successful
physician executive.

The role demands two key elements that cannot be obtained (with
rare exception) without substantial direct experience: clinical insight
and professional leadership competence. *Clinical insight* means personal
understanding and emotional appreciation of the clinician/patient interface. It derives from personal experience with the application of medical
techniques and technology at the individual patient level, with the impact
of disease on individuals and their families and significant others, and with
internalization of the central values and professional passions of clinical

physicians. The acquisition of clinical insight requires experience as a practicing clinician.

There is near-consensus on the importance of clinical experience to the effective physician executive. While notable exceptions exist, physician executives almost always carry clinical experience in their career portfolios. Nonetheless, in recent years, the debate has intensified regarding the necessary extent or duration of that clinical experience, as well as the necessity for currency. As the emergence of the physician executive role accelerated two decades ago, conventional wisdom clearly reflected the central importance of continuing clinical practice for physician executives' credibility with clinical colleagues. In describing one of the first graduate programs for development of physician executives, Detmer and Noren (1981) characterized the clinician executive role as "practicing health professionals . . . who foresee career paths leading to leadership roles" and noted further that the "clinical insight prerequisite is essential to full development for future roles as clinician executives."

While the physician executive continues to face the major challenge of bridging the gap between practicing clinical physicians and management, management expertise increasingly gains currency and value while the field perceives current and continuing clinical expertise as less critical than it was two decades ago. Johnson (1997) notes that "the role model of the independent, well-trained, and experienced clinician (in management) will have disappeared. . . . A decade from now, those who join the ranks of management will do so early in their professional careers." Kirschman (1996) similarly documents that "87 percent of physicians serving in senior management positions have no clinical responsibilities. This is a dramatic change from ten years ago, when half of these managers had clinical duties. The concept of physician executives continuing to do some hands-on clinical work as a means of establishing credibility is fading."

Of course, management complexity and time demands on physician executives principally drive the increasing emphasis on management and decreasing emphasis on clinical practice. However, this does not diminish the importance of the clinical insight described above. This experiential element has far greater importance than its simple value as purchasing power for credibility with practicing clinical physician colleagues. Kindig (1997) characterized the value of clinical insight as "not primarily for the respect of physician peers . . . but mainly the deep and experiential understanding of the medical care process, of the physician/patient relationship, of physician values and culture, of the hidden subtleties of medical ethics, and of the difficulty of the quality/cost tradeoff at the individual patient level." This clinical insight comes from life experience in the clinical arena at some time during the physician executive's career. It does not necessitate current clinical practice, nor does it necessarily require a long period in clinical practice, although insight clearly increases with duration of clinical activity.

The Physician as CEO

Although traditional nonphysician executives occupy most CEO positions in large group practices, managed care organizations, hospitals, and integrated health systems and physician executives usually occupy upper middle management staff functions, an increasing number of physicians have appeared as CEOs in major organizations. LeTourneau and Curry (1997) have analyzed the evolution of physician executives extensively and note that "clinicians, particularly physicians, who learn management skills and develop their leadership skills make the best CEOs and senior leaders of healthcare organizations [and] over the next 10–15 years, we expect to see more clinician CEOs, but not a wholesale shift in that direction." While most future physician executives will serve in senior technical management positions, increasingly they will assume CEO roles. The career paths of physician executives in the future will more closely parallel those of M.B.A. graduates in American industry. Of course, most such graduates serve in midlevel and senior management roles. While only a select few M.B.A. graduates rise to chief executive officer, most corporate CEOs are nonetheless M.B.A. graduates. In the American healthcare industry, few CEOs are physician executives. In the decade ahead, an increasing proportion of healthcare CEOs will be physician executives.

Kirschman (1996) also recognizes this trend, noting, "Physicians are transitioning from technicians to managers, from the doctor managers to the executives who have medicine as a specialty area, not unlike other managers, such as finance and engineering directors."

Consistent with this evolution, the once part-time role of vice president for medical affairs (VPMA) continually becomes more complex and sophisticated, at times now serving as a stepping stone to the role of CEO. Sherer (1993) notes that "many experts agree, the VPMAs of today may very well become the CEOs of tomorrow."

The history of America's world-class technological industries has many parallels to these trends in the physician executive role. For example, the early development and preeminence of the American electronics and computer industries came from executive leadership by people with sophisticated technological background and insights. RCA, IBM, Westinghouse, Control Data, Raytheon, and other corporate success stories carry a common theme of executive leaders providing technological innovation dependent on their personal engineering and technical experiences. Smith (1995) argues that the later failures of these corporate giants, although temporary, were characterized by replacement of technologically sophisticated leadership with more pure management executives.

Smith dramatically illustrates his argument with the disastrous failure of RCA to capitalize on an amazing technological innovation, the liquid crystal display (LCD), by one of its engineers. David Sarnoff, the visionary leader of RCA for 40 years, built the company to "the forefront of the world in communications technology." He created RCA's model of innovation, the David Sarnoff Laboratories, which he considered "the jewel of his corporate crown." Sarnoff was himself very sophisticated technologically, and his insights were a critical element of RCA's innovation and world leadership. George Heilmeier was the engineer at RCA's Sarnoff Lab who invented the LCD. But by the time the LCD was invented, Sarnoff, the premiere technological executive, was almost 80 years old and had relinquished most of his executive responsibilities to others without his technological understanding.

Smith describes RCA's response to the LCD invention as an example of American failure of insightful technical leadership. He says, "What happened to George Heilmeier's invention graphically illustrates why America lost a great deal of its technological leadership and commercial supremacy in key economic sectors in the 1970s and 1980s . . . an episode that has parallels with other American high-tech creations [that] were commercialized by other nations at great cost to both U.S. corporations . . . and millions of American workers, who saw foreigners get the jobs that Americans would have had. . . . RCA was suffering from a loss of vision at the top . . . a gap in technical competence and understanding at the top of the business. RCA, at the time of the LCD invention, was not led by executives with scientific training and technical experience, people with a keen grasp of the technologies that would shape the marketplace of the future. . . . [T]he new breed were managers—marketing men, financial experts, business school graduates—people whose first devotion was to managing corporate stability, not stirring the pot with innovations."

Sharp, the then quite modest Japanese electronics corporation, saw the value of the LCD and capitalized it to overwhelming success at RCA's expense. "What Sharp saw and exploited—which RCA failed to see and exploit—was the enormous potential of the calculator market. . . . The first calculators were crude and inefficient; they ran on batteries, and the batteries were always running out. . . . Once the low-power LCD was perfected, the life of a calculator jumped to a hundred hours. . . ." Sharp's technological insight facilitated its development of LCD applications that "offered a huge competitive advantage in Japan's 'calculator wars' [and] enabled Sharp eventually to move into laptop computer screens and high-definition television. . . ." Smith (1995) explains Sharp's conquest of RCA in the LCD market: "Its leadership was heavily steeped in engineering and therefore quick to grasp the potential of new technologies."

Today's healthcare industry faces unprecedented leadership challenges. Its technological complexity increases continually at a mind-boggling rate. The need for healthcare executives who bring technological insight, training, and experience to the role has never been more critical. The success of America's healthcare system in the twenty-first century will depend on physician executives with technological and clinical insight plus sophisticated management training and experience who will bring innovation to the industry essential to its effective societal purpose. The new leadership order must challenge older healthcare management traditions, organizations, and processes, and development of this new leadership breed necessitates similar innovation in graduate education.

Physician Executive Education

Formal educational programs designed specifically for physician executives began in the late 1970s. Most of these were nondegree programs, notably the well-subscribed and successful "Physician in Management" seminars that the American College of Physician Executives continues to offer today. One of the first formal graduate programs specifically designed for physician executives, a master's of science in administrative medicine, began at the University of Wisconsin in the late 1970s. Using a nontraditional scheduling format, it was targeted not only to physicians but to other clinicians as well and was termed a "clinician executive" program (Detmer and Noren 1981).

Prior to the 1970s, aspiring physician executives who pursued formal education had three conventional degree options (or minor variations on these degree types): M.B.A., master's of health services administration or hospital administration (M.H.A. or M.H.S.A.), and master's of public health (M.P.H.). These programs were largely full-time, on-campus approaches, and they continue to serve a substantial number of physicians. However, executive education programs that are specifically designed for physician executives and use nontraditional scheduling, distance learning, and other methods that adapt to the professional and lifestyle demands of midcareer physicians have increased dramatically during the 1990s.

Although no comprehensive survey of physician executive education has yet been conducted and no single directory of programs exists, the following summary provides the most complete inventory available to date. This program inventory was compiled from several sources, including the *Directory of Programs 1996–1998* of the Association of University Programs in Health Administration (AUPHA), a 1996 survey of physician executive education conducted by the University of Washington, program brochures, and numerous personal communications. AUPHA is the principal American/Canadian association of university-based education programs in health administration, and its directory lists 72 conventional master's degree programs in health administration and 10 executive education programs leading to the master's degree. The ten executive education programs follow nontraditional schedules, and several of the conventional programs offer flexible scheduling options. The University of Washington survey, conducted by Austin Ross, gathered information on seven university graduate programs (Ross 1996).

Standards determination for health administration programs (including those emphasizing physician executive education) occurs principally through the Accrediting Commission on Education for Health Services Administration (ACEHSA), which is recognized as "the only accrediting agency in the field of health services administration . . . the most important assurance for quality developed by the profession and the health services industry" (*Health Services Administration Education Directory of Programs 1996–1998* 1996). It began in 1968 and has 11 sponsors:

- American College of Healthcare Executives
- American College of Medical Practice Executives
- American College of Physician Executives
- American Hospital Association
- American Medical Association
- American Organization of Nurse Executives
- American Public Health Association
- Association of University Programs in Health Administration
- Canadian College of Health Service Executives
- Healthcare Forum
- Healthcare Financial Management Association.

The accreditation process includes preparation of a self-study by the program, site visit and report, accreditation decision, and continuing progress reports. Evaluation addresses eight curriculum content areas:

- Factors influencing use of health services, health status, and determinants of population health

- Organization, financing, and delivery of health services
- Economics, financial policy, and quantitative analysis
- Ethics
- Organizational behavior
- Leadership
- Resource management: human, capital, information
- Quality improvement. (*Handbook of Accreditation Policies and Procedures* 1993)

The following inventory summarizes three types of graduate programs, including both "executive education" approaches using flexible and part-time schedules accommodating working professionals and conventional, on-campus, full-time programs:

Type 1: Exclusive Physician/Clinician Executive Graduate Programs

These are designed exclusively for experienced physicians and other clinical professionals who continue their professional responsibilities and pursue the master's degree part time. Physicians constitute at least 90 percent of students, and all students are clinical professionals. The programs follow nontraditional and flexible schedules, such as weekend, evening, or intensive one- to two-week sessions on campus, as well as teleconferencing, self-study, and other distance learning methods.

Type 2: Mixed Clinician and Nonclinician Executive Graduate Programs

These are designed for both clinical professionals and nonclinicians who continue their professional responsibilities and pursue the master's degree part time. The programs specifically emphasize participation by clinicians, who constitute a substantial proportion of the student participants. The programs follow nontraditional and flexible schedules, such as weekend, evening, or intensive one- to two-week sessions on campus, as well as teleconferencing, self-study, and other distance learning methods.

Type 3: Graduate Programs Not Emphasizing Clinicians

Executive Type

This is open to students of all backgrounds who continue their professional responsibilities and pursue the master's degree part time. The programs have no particular emphasis on clinicians, although clinicians may participate. The programs follow nontraditional and flexible schedules, such as weekend, evening, or intensive one- to two-week sessions on campus, as well as teleconferencing, self-study, and other distance learning methods.

Conventional Type

This is open to students of all backgrounds who pursue the master's degree full time in traditional on-campus schedules.

Tables 4.1 through 4.5 summarize the nature of these three types of graduate education programs. Although programs designed for "exclusive physician/clinician" or "mixed clinician and nonclinician" education (Tables 4.1 and 4.2) most closely match physician executive needs, geographic proximity or other practical considerations might lead some physicians to seek management education through more traditional approaches. Most commonly, those approaches are conventional M.B.A., M.H.A., or M.P.H. programs, or variations on one of these degrees. The 76 health administration programs listed in the directory of the Association of University Programs in Health Administration include all three types. Among these 76 programs, 70 offer conventional full-time, on-campus programs; 16 offer both conventional programs and "executive"-type options that follow flexible schedules, such as weekend, evening, or intensive one- to two-week sessions on campus, as well as teleconferencing, self-study, and other distance learning methods; and 6 of the programs offer only "executive" approaches. Although these 76 graduate programs do not emphasize physician executive education, they nonetheless admit physicians. Tables 4.3 through 4.5 summarize the AUPHA programs, including the types of school in which the programs are located, accreditation, and degrees granted.

The aforementioned 1996 University of Washington survey provides more detailed information for eight physician executive programs. Several common features characterize most of these programs:

- Master's degree
- Class size ranging from 25 to 50
- Predominantly, although not exclusively, physicians
- Students come principally from large healthcare delivery organizations (managed care organizations, hospitals, integrated health systems, group practices)
- Students are typically at midcareer with an average age of about 40
- Programs anticipate increased applications in the next five years
- Tuition averages $27,000 for in-state students and $29,000 for out-of-state students for the full degree program, which is approximately two years in duration
- Nontraditional class schedules using periodic, short, intensive, on-campus sessions often combined with distance education.

Table 4.1 Type 1: Exclusive Physician/Clinician Executive Graduate Programs

Program	Degree	Length	Admission Requirements and Student Type Emphasized	Curriculum Design and Teaching Approach
New York University Advanced Management Program for Clinicians	M.S.	Four semesters	"Clinical professionals . . . holding a postgraduate degree or extensive managerial experience" (Smith 1995).	Program individually tailored with faculty advisor, comprising nine courses, two-semester health policy seminar, and a final paper or project.
Tulane University Master of Medical Management	Master's	Varies	"Physicians committed to management as a major element of their professional careers" (Smith 1995).	Three on-campus, one-week sessions plus off-campus periods of learning and project completion.
University of Houston–Clear Lake M.B.A. for Physicians	M.B.A.	Two years	Physicians	13 modules, on campus every other Friday/Saturday plus two two-week sessions and one one-week session on campus.
University of South Florida M.B.A. Program for Physicians	M.B.A.	21 months	Physicians	20 courses.
University of Wisconsin Administrative Medicine Program	M.S.	22 months	"Physicians and nurses . . . with clinical and managerial experience" (Smith 1995)	Nonresidential program, six one-week on-campus sessions, weekly teleconferences, one-week executive preceptorship, 15 hours of home study per week.

Table 4.2 Type 2: Mixed Clinician and Nonclinician Executive Graduate Programs

Program	Degree	Length	Admission Requirements and Student Type Emphasized	Curriculum Design and Teaching Approach
University of Colorado/Network for Healthcare Management Executive Program in Health Administration	M.S.	25 months	"Health care managers and clinicians currently working in provider organizations" with at least three years' experience (Smith 1995).	Five sessions on campus plus computer conferencing off campus—designed to facilitate education while students remain in their careers.
Medical College of Virginia Executive M.S. Program in Health Administration	M.S.H.A.	Two years	"Clinicians, . . . executive- [or] mid-level managers . . . technical specialists . . . in health . . . or . . . other industries" with five years' professional experience (Smith 1995).	Five on-campus sessions, 7–11 days each plus four semesters five-and-a-half months long using computer conferencing, computer-aided and programmed instruction, 15–20 hours of study per week.
University of Miami Executive M.B.A.	M.B.A.	Two years	"Business professionals and clinicians" with two to five years of management experience (Smith 1995).	On-campus sessions 45 Saturdays per year for two years.
University of Michigan On Job/On Campus Program, School of Public Health	M.P.H. or M.H.S.A.	25 months	"Physicians, professionals from nursing, law, dentistry, finance, pharmacy, and general management" with three years' healthcare experience (Smith 1995).	On campus four days every four to five weeks—all students "must remain employed while in the program."

continued

Table 4.2 *Continued*

Program	Degree	Length	Admission Requirements and Student Type Emphasized	Curriculum Design and Teaching Approach
University of North Carolina–Chapel Hill Executive Master's in Health Policy and Administration	M.H.A. or M.P.H.	Varies	"Employed health professionals and health administrators [with] bachelor's degree and three years' prior experience in health administration or a health profession" (Smith 1995).	Part-time graduate study using off-campus instruction, summer school courses, distance learning, and home-based studies.
University of Washington School of Public Health Extended M.P.H.	M.P.H.	Three years	"Midcareer public, community, or environmental health professionals" (Smith 1995).	Three on-campus four-week summer sessions, directed independent study, four on-campus weekend seminars, independent and group projects, and electives.

Table 4.3 Type 3: Executive Graduate Programs Not Emphasizing Clinicians

Program	Degree	Length	Student Type Emphasized	Curriculum Design and Teaching Approach
City University of New York	M.B.A.	Three years	Part-time exclusively	18 credits per year for three years.
Clark University/ University of Massachusetts Medical School	M.H.A.	2 years plus field experience	"Significant prior health field experience . . . currently employed in health professions" (Smith 1995).	19 courses part-time.
Cleveland State University	M.B.A.	39 months	"Part-time learner currently employed" (Smith 1995).	Course usually offered in the evening.
Governors State University	M.H.A.	2 years	"Employed, studying part-time, and career-oriented" (Smith 1995).	Most classes held late afternoon and early evening.
Hartford Graduate Center	M.S.	varies: total req. 31 credits	"Entirely . . . part-time students who are working in health care or related fields . . . two to ten years' experience" (Smith 1995).	Both full time and adjunct faculty with backgrounds in healthcare management.
Medical College of South Carolina	M.H.A.	2 years	"Health professionals or individuals employed in health or health-related institutions" (Smith 1995).	Courses evening and some weekends.
University of New Hampshire	M.H.A.	21 months	"Currently working in the field of health services . . . continuing to work full time" (Smith 1995).	Alternate weekends plus two residential weeks.

continued

Table 4.3 *Continued*

Program	Degree	Length	Student Type Emphasized	Curriculum Design and Teaching Approach
New York University Saturday M.P.A. Program	M.P.A.	Three years	"Open to any individual holding a bachelor's degree or first professional degree" (Smith 1995).	On campus every Saturday fall and spring semester for three years.
University of St. Thomas	M.H.A.	35 months	"Functioning as clinic or medical group managers [and] those who would enter this area" (Smith 1995).	Two formats: campus-based weekend model and off-campus, distance learning model.
University of Scranton	M.H.A.	30 months	"Currently working in the health care industry . . . pursue graduate studies while continuing to work full time" (Smith 1995).	Evening courses.
Simmons College	M.S.	42 months	"Working professionals who attend school part time" (Smith 1995).	All courses taught early evening.
University of Southern California	M.H.A.	30 months	"Established professionals . . . employed" (Smith 1995).	All-day sessions in or around weekends.
University of Toronto	M.H.Sc.	22 months	"Currently employed" (Smith 1995).	Wednesday evening through Saturday once monthly.

continued

Table 4.3 *Continued*

Program	Degree	Length	Student Type Emphasized	Curriculum Design and Teaching Approach
Trinity University Individual Study Program in Health Administration	M.B.A.	Three years	"Individuals currently holding responsible positions in a health care organization [with] prior management-level experience" and a baccalaureate degree.	Each semester starts with three-day on-campus session followed by home study and regular teleconferencing sessions.
Widener University	M.H.A.	41 months Three years	"Individuals wishing to continue their employment while working for their graduate degree" (Smith 1995).	Courses primarily in evening hours.
Xavier University	M.H.A.	Three years	"Working professional" (Smith 1995).	Two evenings per week plus residency assignment in the student's place of work.

Table 4.4 Summary of All AUPHA Graduate Programs, Number, School Type, Accreditation

AUPHA School Member Conventional Programs	ACEHSA* Accredited	AACSB† Accredited	CEPH‡ Accredited	LCME** Accredited	Other and/or Accredited
76	68	24	16	12	11

*Accrediting Commission on Education for Health Services Administration
†American Association of Colleges and Schools of Business
‡Council on Education in Public Health
**Liaison Committee on Medical Education

Table 4.5 Degrees Granted by AUPHA Graduate Programs

Degree	M.H.A.*	M.B.A.	M.P.H.	M.S./M.A.	Other
Number†	42	24	10	14	4

*Includes M.S.H.A. and M.H.S.A. or equivalent degree.
†Total degrees exceed number of programs because several programs grant more than one degree.

Table 4.6 summarizes the specific details of these surveyed programs and of the proposed new University of Washington program.

Although 68 of the 76 graduate programs listed in the AUPHA directory have ACEHSA accreditation, only one "exclusive physician/clinician executive graduate program" (University of Wisconsin) and four "mixed clinician and nonclinician executive graduate programs" (Medical College of Virginia, University of Colorado, University of Miami, and University of North Carolina) have been awarded ACEHSA accreditation.

Conclusions

The change rate and complexity of the American healthcare system in the twenty-first century poses leadership challenges requiring a new breed of executive. The portfolio of talents and expertise demanded of this new executive has few parallels in the history of American industry. The explosive growth and central importance of the computer and electronics industries at the emergence of the "information age" represent the best parallel. However, the leading healthcare executive of the future will

Table 4.6 University of Washington Survey of Physician Executive Education

Program	Degree	Size	Tuition for Full Degree Program	Length	School in the University	Percentage Physicians	Years in Existence	Average Age of Physicians	Trend in Enrollment	Design
Executive on-campus Program in Health Administration, University of Colorado, Denver	M.S.H.A.	36–45	$28,000	25 months	School of Business	30–50%	Ten years	40–50	Up 15–30%	Intensive every six months (total ten weeks) plus distance education.
Management Education Program for Physicians in Leadership Positions, University of Colorado	No degree —short courses and seminars only	Varies	Varies	Varies	School of Business	30–50%	Ten years		Up	Short sessions two hours to three days.
M.B.A. Program for Physicians, University of South Florida	M.B.A.	40	$28,975 in-state $35,850 out of state	21 months	School of Business	100%	Five years	44	Up	20 courses.

continued

Table 4.6 *Continued*

Program	Degree	Size	Tuition for Full Degree Program	Length	School in the University	Percentage Physicians	Years in Existence	Average Age of Physicians	Trend in Enrollment	Design
Master of Science Administrative Medicine, University of Wisconsin–Madison	M.S.	25	$28,700	22 months	Medical School	90%	17 years	42	Up	Nonresidential distance education plus six on-campus sessions (nine weeks total on campus).
Health Administration Program, University of Kentucky	M.H.A.	25	$5,628 in-state $15,548 out of state	Four semesters	School of Public Administration and School of Allied Health	3%	Five years	30	Up	On-campus, four-semester program.
M.B.A. for Physicians, University of Houston–Clear Lake	M.B.A.	15	$25,000 in-state $30,755 out of state	Two years	School of Business	100%	One year	40	Up	13 modules: on-campus every other Friday/Saturday plus two two-week sessions and one one-week session.

continued

Table 4.6 *Continued*

Program	Degree	Size	Tuition for Full Degree Program	Length	School in the University	Percentage Physicians	Years in Existence	Average Age of Physicians	Trend in Enrollment	Design
Health Services Management Program, Kellogg Graduate School of Management, Northwestern University	M.B.A. (MM)	20–60	$42,000	Varies	School of Business	15–20%	50 years	25–50	Up	Degree program, custom-designed programs for healthcare organizations, vary from three days to multiple week-long continuing education programs per year.
University of Washington Evening Executive M.H.A. Program (Proposed)	M.H.A.	25–30		Three years	School of Public Health	Est. most are physicians	New			Nonresidential, evening classes, distance learning, e-mail networking, teleconferencing, video instruction.

need additional strengths. Like executives in the cutting-edge "information age" industries, these executives must acquire deep technological insights, sophisticated management expertise, a thorough understanding of complicated data analysis, and a futuristic vision. Additionally, the leading executive must bring a special human element, clinical insight, as well as a humanitarian orientation, none of which hold central positions in the leadership of the computer and electronics industries. These unique elements of the healthcare industry will drive dependence on physician executives and clinician executives to fill midlevel and senior management roles as well as the CEO ranks of the healthcare system of the next century.

Graduate programs must respond to the need of physician executives through innovative approaches that accommodate the schedules and lifestyles of the student population, typically older, midcareer physicians with substantial professional experience as clinicians and modest but growing managerial responsibilities. Conventional business skills and education programs do not satisfy the specialized need in either content or teaching methods. This special need dictates distance education approaches, nontraditional schedules, practical applicability to real-world clinical delivery organizations coupled with thorough theoretical/disciplinary treatment, and faculty who possess academic expertise and direct management experience. It is very important that the programs capitalize on the value of the interchange among the students and the wealth of experience they bring to the learning process. Finally, for the new physician executive, the graduate program must serve as a beginning rather than a capstone of preparation for leadership, given the dynamic state of the healthcare system and the complexity of transition from clinical physician to executive.

Few would question the intellectual capacities of the physician and clinician cadre in American healthcare. However, the translation from clinical expertise to executive leadership poses a formidable challenge to both current physician leaders and graduate education programs that must respond to the profound need for leadership.

References

Detmer, D., and J. Noren. 1981. "An Administrative Medicine Program for Clinician Executives." *Journal of Medical Education* 56 (8): 640–45.

Dunham, N., D. Kindig, and R. Schultz. 1994. "The Value of the Physician Executive Role to Organizational Effectiveness and Performance." *Healthcare Management Review* 19 (4): 56–63.

Handbook of Accreditation Policies and Procedures. 1993. Arlington, VA: Accrediting Commission on Education for Health Services Administration.

Health Services Administration Education Directory of Programs 1996–1998. 1996. Arlington, VA: Association of University Programs in Health Administration.

Johnson, R. 1997. "Physicians as Executives: Barriers to Success." *Frontiers of Health Services Management* 13 (3): 28–32.

Kindig, D. 1997. "Do Physician Executives Make a Difference?" *Frontiers of Health Services Management* 13 (3): 38–42.

Kirschman, D. 1996. "Physician Executives Share Insights." *Physician Executive* 22 (9): 27–30.

Kurtz, M. 1994. "The Dual Role Dilemma." In *New Leadership in Healthcare Management: The Physician Executive*, 2nd Ed., edited by W. Curry. Tampa, FL: American College of Physician Executives.

Lee, P., and C. Estes. 1997. *The Nation's Health*. Sudbury, MA: Jones and Bartlett.

LeTourneau, B., and W. Curry. 1997. "Physicians as Executives: Boon or Boondoggle?" *Frontiers of Health Services Management* 13 (3): 3–25, 43–45.

Linney, G., and B. Linney. 1992. *Medical Directors: What. Why. How*. Tampa, FL: American College of Physician Executives.

Ross, A. 1996. Personal communication, January 19.

Sherer, J. 1993. "Medical Execs Rising—Today's VPMAs Are High-Profile and Strategy Savvy." *Hospitals* 67 (4): 48–51.

Smith, H. 1995. *Rethinking America*. New York: Random House.

Starr, P. 1982. *The Social Transformation of American Medicine*. New York: Basic Books.

Further Reading

Cummings, K. 1988. "Why Some Managers Fail." *Physician Executive* 14 (4): 6–8.

Lloyd, J. 1994. "What Kind of Leaders Will Be Successful?" *Physician Executive* 20 (3): 8–11.

Weil, T. 1997. "Physician Executives: Additional Factors Impinging on Their Future Success." *Frontiers of Health Services Management* 13 (3): 33–37.

Managing the Transition from Clinician to Manager and Leader

Sandra L. Gill

THIS CHAPTER examines the differences between leadership skills and competencies derived from clinical practice. Specifically, three issues are addressed:
1. skill sets that enhance organizational leadership roles;
2. preparing the clinician for management roles; and
3. career transition preparation and pitfalls.

Leadership Role Variation and Its Consequences

Today, physician executives enjoy a well-established leadership role—one with remarkably high internal role variation. That physician leaders are important is rarely debated. Joint Commission on Accreditation of Healthcare Organizations (JCAHO) accreditation requirements incorporate medical staff leaders as part of the acute care hospital leadership group, along with nurses, administrators/executives, and members of the governing board (*Comprehensive Accreditation Manual for Hospitals* 1997). Formal involvement of physicians in health system integration has been empirically identified as one of the three building blocks of a value-added, robust healthcare delivery system in which integration of physicians is significantly related to higher patient care productivity and higher levels of clinical integration (Shortell et al. 1996).

While the growth of physicians in formal leadership roles has been significant, it is still characterized by wide role variation. For example, Kindig identified more than 168,000 physician executives in 1986, counting those whose administrative work hours ranged from less than 45 hours to more than 65 hours per week (Kindig 1997). This represented a growth of 39 percent in the decade from 1976 to 1986. Of the nearly 12,000 current members of the American College of Physician Executives, more than 60 percent function as physician executives in three major organizational settings: hospitals (27.1 percent); group practices (23.1 percent) and managed care (10.6 percent) (LeTourneau and Curry 1997). Others function in a variety of for-profit and not-for-profit settings, including health systems, military roles, consulting, ambulatory care centers, insurance, and industrial settings. Thus, making the transition from clinician to manager requires a special sensitivity to the extraordinary variety of currently reported organizational roles.

Even within the same organization, such as a hospital, physicians will encounter significant role differentiation. For example, the elected medical staff president has a set of responsibilities different from those of the hospital-based clinical department medical director. Indeed, the term *medical director* often includes the hospital-based clinical department director as well as the hospitalwide medical director or vice president for medical affairs (VPMA).

The wide variation in role expectations for physician executives complicates making the transition, because it stands in such stark contrast to the physician's preparation for his or her medical degree. Rather than being a defined, highly competitive progression of cognitive and behavioral skills, the transition from clinician to manager can occur almost overnight. Furthermore, role requirements vary so widely that even experienced physician executives reach the same level of responsibility from entirely different career paths, with varying skills and abilities.

To date, the physician leadership literature is based on normative traits of basic responsibilities, rather than on a definitive set of role competencies associated with strict professional entrance requirements. This trait-based description of role responsibilities in the physician leadership literature trails organizational leadership research and trends by almost 20 years, which calls for much more rigorous research about physicians in leadership roles (Gill 1977).

Skill Sets for Physician Managers

Seven major skill sets emerge from the current literature, which is admittedly based on survey research and qualitative reports of current physician leaders. At a glance, these skill sets include clinical competence; interpersonal skills; personal management competencies; basic skills in use of computers, information technology, and healthcare applications; quality management skill; system thinking and organizational design applications; and transformational leadership competencies.

Clinical Competence

Given the lack of definitive competencies for physician leaders to acquire, there is a broad normative calling for certain skills and abilities (Kirschman and Grebenschikoff 1997). Although exceptions can be found, one emerging trend is toward the requirement for clinical experience (Williams and Ewell 1996). For example, the American Board of Medical Management and the Administrative Medical Program at the University of Wisconsin–Madison require clinical board certification (Kindig 1997). Kirschman and Grebenschikoff (1997) report that 95 percent of physician executives currently in senior-level positions are board certified and that virtually all executive search criteria stipulate board certification. With the increasing penetration of managed care, clinical board certification is becoming a common indicator of clinical quality. We can expect this requirement to grow as a prerequisite for physician managers as role models.

For physician managers clinical competence is typically demonstrated by a number of years in clinical practice along with leadership roles in quality and other clinical initiatives. Chief of staff, major department chair tenure, residency program directorships, and medical directorships in physician organizations and managed care organizations are all common experiential development for contemporary physician managers. Thus, while clinical training is emerging as a prerequisite for physician managers, previous experience in significant organizational leadership roles is also necessary. Advanced educational opportunities in business and organizational management is often acquired during one's management tenure.

Interpersonal Skills

In addition to specific clinical skills, such as quality management, credentialing, healthcare regulatory compliance, physician recruitment, and medical education and supervision, the current literature reflects great emphasis on interpersonal competence (Kindig 1997; Kirschman and Grebenschikoff 1997). Generally called "effective communication skills," the interpersonal package encompasses effective oral communication; relationships with key stakeholders, the public, and various media; and written communication. It extends to being able to exert appropriate influence with others, including persuasion, ability to motivate others, serving as liaison between various groups, and resolving conflicts (Kirschman and Grebenschikoff 1997; Williams and Ewell 1996; Linney and Linney 1992).

Of particular note for physician managers is how fragile their role authority may be. In contrast to the credibility a practicing physician has by virtue of being a physician, the physician executive is often relegated to a negative stereotype, seen, perhaps, as "another suit." Other physicians may disdain the physician manager as one who has departed from an honorable calling, and nonphysician managers may see the physician manager as a threat (LeTourneau and Curry 1997). Interpersonal competence, especially in terms of building effective work relationships, becomes even more critical when one's formal role authority is not firmly held. Powerful role authority protects and deflects criticism, but physician executives have to overcome negative role stereotypes. It requires even more interpersonal competence.

Interpersonal competence—the skills to work within an organizational setting where one is among other leaders, rather than the leader—is essential (Cummings 1998). In addition to clinical initiatives, physician managers can expect to fulfill administrative functions. Many of the administrative assignments include "boundary spanning," i.e., working collaboratively with others, especially where the manager does not have formal hierarchical authority. The effective boundary spanner uses interpersonal skills to establish effective relationships, rather than relying on formal organizational authority (Kindig and Kovner 1992).

McCall's (1990) examination of why physician leaders fail also addressed the importance of interpersonal skills. In no particular order, McCall cited "ten deadly flaws of physician managers": insensitivity and arrogance, inability to choose staff, overmanaging (inability to delegate), inability to adapt to a boss, fighting the wrong battles, being seen as untrustworthy (having questionable motives), failing to develop a strategic vision, being overwhelmed by the job, lacking specific skills or knowledge, and lacking commitment to the job. McCall quotes a senior physician executive as saying, "It's almost always people management that does them in."

Personal Management Competencies

A third cadre of skills relates to personal management capacities. Specifically, time management, the ability to establish and attain goals, and the ability to manage one's emotions are indicated both in the literature and in repeated interactions with experienced physician managers. Time management is the result of being thrust into a complex, turbulent organizational environment in which the typical physician manager assumes multiple, often conflicting leadership roles. Physicians who may have grown accustomed to operating on a daily schedule of patient care appointments may have considerable difficulty adjusting to large group meetings and long-term projects in which they must facilitate others' participation and task completion. The physician manager will simply not have time to interact one-to-one as much as he or she desires. The ability to manage one's time appropriately to the needs of the organization as well as with some personal satisfaction is a well-documented challenge. Physicians who may have exceptional efficiencies as individuals often report frustration with the slow, circular, and often vague outcomes of management in complex organizations, so most physicians can expect adjustments in their expectations of time and accomplishments.

Personal goal setting is important to maintain one's sense of perspective and personal and professional growth. Covey (1989) describes the importance of recognizing one's "zone of influence," in which a personal action can make a difference, in contrast to the broader "zone of concern," in which one has a concern but little likelihood of actual influence. Setting reasonable goals, maintaining awareness of one's zone of influence, and committing to important but not immediately urgent goals are characteristics of highly effective people.

Emotional competence has been cited in the physician leadership literature as a potential source of management failure (Cummings 1988). Personal realities for physician managers include significant frustration, potential impatience with organizational complexities, and the necessity to work in group and team settings. These conditions may be in stark contrast to the practicing clinician's work environment. Furthermore, the physician's clinical practice pattern of face-to-face interactions may become suddenly transformed into large group settings. Not only are large groups more complex than one-to-one relationships, but they typically require more facilitation and group maintenance than the close, personal contact of doctor-doctor, doctor-patient, and doctor-nurse dynamics (Shull et al. 1970).

Personality theory and research also suggests that highly introverted personalities, who thrive in close face to face relationships, may feel their personal energies dissipate in the very large group setting, whereas extroverted personalities seem to thrive (Jung 1971). Many management roles, by definition, require extensive large group interactions, leaving highly introverted leaders desperate for some quiet, private space in which to restore their sense of personal energy and creativity.

Finally, physician managers may not maintain sufficient behaviors that demonstrate concern for others. Because this is often a function of others' perceptions, physician managers must attend to how they communicate nonverbally to others. Executive training seminars, mentoring, and personal feedback exercises are all incorporated in management development efforts to heighten personal awareness and more congruent communication skills. Communication research on high-risk conditions demonstrates the importance of leaders' communicating empathy, trustworthiness, and credibility (Covello 1991). Recent leadership research also connects individual, personal behavior with perceptions of managers' credibility (Kouzes and Posner 1993). Burning bridges as a private practicing physician may be overcome through one's clinical expertise. As a manager, it will become a career-limiting act!

Computer Literacy and Information System Skills

The fourth group of competencies reflects more technical skills, including computers and informatics (LeTourneau and Curry 1997; Grebenschikoff 1995). Recognition that healthcare organizations will increasingly be defined by their information systems hastens the need for personal knowledge and skills in information system software, systems design, and clinical applications. The rapid transformation of manual to electronic information applications requires basic computer literacy, at a minimum. Increasing use of the Internet and of health system intranets for group communications across geographically distant organizational sites for real-time problem solving, clinical applications, and education require additional electronic skills and experience. Physician managers can expect to interact with others through electronic media, including telemedicine, video conferencing, and intranet and Internet applications. Experience in these forums will be essential for physician managers now and in the future.

Quality Improvement and Management Applications

A fifth group of clinical applications skills is now a prerequisite set of leadership experiences for the contemporary physician leader and full-time manager, including quality improvement concepts and techniques, utilization review, clinical pathway development, quality management and clinical outcomes, and community health and disease management technologies (LeTourneau and Curry 1997; Grebenschikoff 1995). While these basic quality applications are essential at the management level, experience in them to achieve accreditation goals is desirable. In addition to acute care JCAHO accreditation, physician managers can expect to become involved in NCQA accreditation and should seek appropriate training to prepare for this experience.

Physician managers need to be prepared to identify, help evaluate, pilot test, and endorse a wide variety of quality improvement efforts across the continuum of care, in health system integration efforts and in community health status improvement. Veloski and colleagues, in their analysis of medical student education in managed care settings, described competencies necessary for future physicians to practice effectively in a managed care setting (Veloski 1996). These competencies include expanded primary care skills for generalist physicians and other topics the authors argue are relevant for all physicians, including healthcare organization and finance, resource allocation and risk management, quantitative methods related to the health of populations, health services research skills, computer applications and medical informatics, social and behavioral sciences, and medical ethics. If practicing physicians need these skills for their futures, we suggest that physician managers will need to accelerate their acquisition of them as leaders of healthcare organizations in a managed care environment. Furthermore, knowledge and skill in the application of quality principles in managed care settings, especially capitated care, requires additional understanding of managed care insurance, risk management, actuarial, and financial concepts and techniques (Kongstvedt 1995).

This scope of skills, so much larger than those of direct doctor-patient interactions in an illness episode, requires system thinking and creativity to translate from patient care to community health and prevention goals.

System Thinking and Organizational Design

Postmodernism has influenced management and organizational theory as well as philosophy, economics, art, and literature. Essentially, contemporary thinkers challenge the many assumptions from the Enlightenment, from which the scientific model and belief in rationalism has permeated almost every aspect of our lives for the past 250 years. Postmodernists assert that the methods of logical positivism, in which scientific analyses reduced objects of inquiry to various parts and discrete processes, have failed to recognize more natural truths and phenomena, including the self-organizing properties of living systems. The microanalytic preference of scientific rationalism, according to postmodernists, fails to observe essential system properties, paradoxical relationships, and essential interactions necessary to solve contemporary, complex problems (Cahoone 1996). As Einstein is reported to have said, "Our thinking has created problems that we cannot solve except to get beyond our thinking."

One influence of postmodern thinking about organizations and leadership is an emphasis on whole, dynamic systems. Popularized by Senge (1990) and Wheatley (1992), system thinking looks for patterns and cycles of events, relations between system elements, boundary characteristics (e.g., open, closed, permeable), and nesting of current systems within larger frameworks (McWhinney 1993). Especially important are the unintended consequences of particular organizational leadership actions, which Senge and colleagues (1994) name "fixes that backfire." Thus, contemporary managers are encouraged to learn system design skills to accomplish outcomes that more discrete efforts fail to achieve or that undermine intended results (Nadler, Shaw, and Walton 1995).

Physician managers, for example, would encourage the examination of long-term consequences of particular policies. A short-term incentive strategy to encourage physicians' completion of medical records might actually encourage delinquencies in order to partake in the incentive program for record completion. In other healthcare settings, a system view on hip replacements, across the continuum of care, includes home risk appraisal to make sure that frayed rugs, broken steps, or other household details do not cause reinjury for the senior whose broken hip has just been replaced. Through home-based care, rehabilitation therapy is combined with postoperative follow-up, reducing total case costs and improving patient satisfaction and recovery. For physician managers, system design skills include, at a minimum, thinking through an interdisciplinary continuum of care for clinical services.

Transformational Leadership Competencies

As a consequence of system integration and consolidation among healthcare systems, recent literature has focused on the importance of transformational leadership skills. Burns (1978) distinguished transactional leaders from transformational leaders. Whereas the former engage in relationships with subordinates in a bargaining relationship, transformational leaders engage in more motivational relationships, seeking motives and satisfying higher needs. Kotter (1990) distinguishes *management* from *leadership*, and why both are necessary for complex organizations in changing environments. Management has traditionally focused on the core functions of planning and budgeting; organizing and staffing; and control, including problem solving, monitoring results, and organizing to solve problems resulting from plan deviations. Leadership, in contrast, is embedded in a belief in *constructive or adaptive change*, which focuses on the three subprocesses Kotter calls "establishing direction," "aligning people," and "motivating and inspiring."

Transformational leaders are often engaged in defining a new organizational vision, creating radical organizational change, and inspiring others to achieve extraordinary results (Kouzes and Posner 1988). Indeed, Lloyd (1994) identified six transformational competencies and values critical for twenty-first century healthcare organizations: mastering change, systems thinking, shared vision, continuous quality improvement, redefining healthcare, and improving public and community health status. These qualities are also noted by Shortell et al. (1996) and Gill (1997). In particular, physician managers will need to learn the various skills of strategic planning (Silbiger 1993), competitive strategy (Porter 1980), business planning, and leading change (Kotter 1996). Leadership skills, group facilitation techniques, and organizational planning concepts and skills are all necessary to achieve transformational leadership. Additional personal, interpersonal, team, and organizational factors also influence effective leadership.

For physician managers, this requires a broad understanding of the larger context of healthcare. Finance, healthcare economics, and the related financial impact of managed care have more recently emerged as being essential for the dedicated physician manager (Kirschman 1996). Although there is still debate about the necessity of an M.B.A., the emphasis on acquiring business management skills is widely reflected in various executive development curricula targeted for physicians and within more formal physician executive training programs (Kindig 1997).

A grounding in the overall delivery system elements, along with management and organizational theory, can become the springboard for transformational leadership. For some physicians, this requires overcoming negative attitudes about the value of the social sciences. The "softer side" of management derives from a smorgasbord of sociology; social psychology; management science; and organizational behavior, development, and theory, to name a few. Healthcare and management seem particularly susceptible to "fads" about which the scientifically trained physician is appropriately skeptical. Nevertheless, understanding the applied scientific underpinnings of individual, group, organizational, and system behavior and of change management provides an excellent foundation for physician managers to develop their leadership skills. In other words, clinical competence is necessary but not sufficient for effective physician managers. Management and leadership competence is also required.

Preparing the Clinician for Organizational Leadership

Most clinicians migrate from their clinical roles into medical leadership through early leadership experience on hospital medical staffs or in teaching hospitals. Significant role variation factors contribute to a confusing career path in which almost any entry point can quite serendipitously lead to a management role. In contrast to the more defined requirements for medical education, this contributes to a perception that medical leadership is less rigorous, less professional, and less demanding of skills. Experienced physician executives consistently mention the rigorous demands on physician leaders and the importance of preparation (LeTourneau and Curry 1997).

Research on physician participation in professional development provides some useful insights for preparing physician managers. First, physicians' learning styles will be focused more on a preference for concrete, sequential instructional design, so management development opportunities should recognize that reading, experiential learning, observing role models, and individual skill development need to be provided in addition to formal instructional sessions (Vanvoorhees et al. 1988). Physicians, from their clinical preparations, express an interest in practical applications. Links to patient care remain a high priority in management development curricula. Opportunities for collegial interaction, even recreation and leisure, have been noted in the literature (Cervero 1981). Of particular note is emerging research about women's preference for collaborative interactions in which they can validate their personal experiences (Belenky, Clinchy, and Goldberger 1986).

Health systems report a variety of methods and opportunities to prepare physicians for future leadership roles (Gill 1997). In addition to basic orientation to current leadership functions, many health systems offer tuition for role-related educational seminars. Specific development in quality improvement, total quality management concepts and practices, credentialing, and medical leadership are often provided. These programs are usually offered in off-site seminars, accredited for Category I or II CME credits, and provide participating physicians an opportunity to interact with other physician leaders from a variety of sites and locations.

Where the VPMA position already exists in the healthcare system, more intensive development efforts occur. In addition to coaching and mentoring individual physician leaders on particular problems, the VPMA has the task of developing more formal physician leadership development programs, and VPMAs report numerous management development efforts. Some establish an annual leadership development conference or retreat, typically including all current and incoming elected and appointed physician leaders. In addition, small groups of 7 to 20 "emerging leaders" may be identified and groomed for future leadership roles. They are grouped into an annual class and then participate in off-site seminars and courses, including executive management and M.B.A. courses. Each year, a new "class" of physician leaders is identified, which establishes expectations and support for ongoing management development. Health systems increasingly are developing formal educational programs and curricula for physicians, resulting in academic degrees and certificates (Totten and Orlikoff 1996).

The content of a progressive sequence of management development courses moves, as expected, from concrete basic skills to management and leadership concepts and skills. Basic retreats and seminars usually focus on specific role content to orient the new physician leader to his or her role. For example, orientation to medical staff, health system and hospital functions, JCAHO requirements, credentialing concepts and processes, utilization review, quality improvement concepts and practices, and meeting leadership are common basic orientation topics. Medical director courses and topics shift to business and health system management. Financial analysis, quality outcomes and measurement methods, medical informatics, quantitative planning and resource allocation methods, change management, and media relations are common topics. Specific coaching and mentoring may be added, incorporating experiential training around case studies, role playing, and small group exercises. Use of the Internet is often incorporated to achieve course continuity, complete program requirements, establish and seek mentoring and collegial advice, and create "learning communities" among program participants.

In summary, three common elements seem to characterize the wide variety of preparation routes for physician managers: experience, training, and management competence. Experience is usually denoted by holding elected and appointed leadership offices and roles. Training increasingly requires formal course work, and management competence refers to demonstrated results, such as significant quality improvement, managed care organizational or product development, or utilization management results. Not unlike current standards for clinical privileging, relevant experience, acquired training, and demonstrated results *as a physician leader* are expected. Formal management development, as offered by the American College of Physician Executives, in advanced degree programs, and in various accredited certificate programs, is becoming a prerequisite for senior physician management roles and opportunities.

Career Transition: Preparation and Pitfalls
Personal Transition

Career transition, in any setting, is a complex process, involving professional, emotional, and strategic challenges (Hudson 1991; Bridges 1980). Physicians often report concern that they cannot transition from anything other than clinical practice, "because that's the only thing I'm trained to do." As with any transition, the first step begins with envisioning the possibility of a transition (Striano 1988). Fortunately, thousands of physician managers have created successful career transitions and can help mentor the transition. Interaction with them is a major stimulant, available through the American College of Physician Executives and in health systems, university and hospital settings, managed care organizations, and even consulting firms.

Preparing the Organization for a Physician Manager

Within the local organization, a combination of steps seems critical. First, establishing a shared vision of role and responsibilities is important. Because most physician managers function as part of the organization's executive/administrative team, it will be critical to differentiate the physician manager's role from existing management functions and turf. Determining the nature of the role—"line" supervisory responsibilities or a "staff" function—will be essential, because this often requires a change in organizational reporting relationships. Where physicians have informally functioned as medical directors, formal role development will undoubtedly create tension and conflict. Many physicians perceive that they are providing physician management services on a voluntary basis and resent a new medical director's salary for what appears to be the same kind of work. Other medical directors and vice presidents may have overlapping responsibilities that have to be considered. Contractual agreements with existing physician groups may also be affected when a medical director role is created without consideration of existing contracts. Some physicians may simply abandon their leadership roles on appointment of a paid medical director, because he or she is "getting paid to do this."

After the core functions and responsibilities are developed, identification of requisite skills needs to be established, along with specification of authority and accountability. These factors are usually covered in executive position descriptions for other roles and can be adapted for the physician manager. In addition, we highly recommend that external examples be incorporated, such as position descriptions available from Physician Executive Management Center publications, the Medical Group Management Association, and other physician executive search firms that have solid experience with physician managers and executives. We have witnessed how lack of attention to these basic considerations contributes to early failures, which have long-term consequences for the physician manager and for subsequent attempts to establish the physician executive role.

National and regional norms are available regarding salary and benefits for a variety of physician executive functions (Kirschman and Grebenschikoff 1997). Median total compensation, including base salary and bonus, is $170,000 for senior medical managers; base salary median is $155,000, for a 46-hour workweek, for a physician manager with clinical board certification and four years in his or her current role. One third of respondents in the Physician Executive Management Center survey reported having or working on an advanced management degree (Kirschman and Grebenschikoff 1997). Hospital-based senior medical managers report a longer workweek, and hospital bed size affects compensation levels.

Using these more objective data, along with local ranges, can help substantiate an appropriate salary range. Most physicians will be required to make substantial changes in their practices, either closing them, assuming limited part-time roles, or leaving private practice entirely. Kirschman and Grebenschikoff report a decline in full-time physician executives who maintain a clinical practice: "In most situations, physician executives are just too busy to do justice to clinical practice" (Kirschman and Grebenschikoff 1997). Leaving clinical practice has financial, personal, and symbolic impacts and will not be easy to reverse. Therefore, very careful attention to the development of the physician manager's role and function seem prudent.

A particular concern is the physician manager who appears to have been given his role as a special favor rather than on the basis of competence. The use of an external search consultant to evaluate candidates and make recommendations can be very helpful even with a single applicant. It is quite common for the first medical director or vice president for medical affairs to arise from the organization's medical staff, after years of clinical and leadership experience. Nevertheless, installing even a well-known physician in a management role without adequate evaluation of his or her competence can create a demeaning role perception that eviscerates potential influence and success.

Another consideration is effective performance evaluation. In many hospital settings, evaluation of medical directors has been neglected. Many considerations require that physician managers be evaluated as rigorously as other managers. In anticipation of performance evaluation, physician managers will be encouraged to establish goals and focus on organizational results. It also stimulates useful discussion with the physician manager's superior about relevant needs and aspirations, professional and organizational development, and communication. New physician managers, in particular, should establish a professional development plan to acquire formal training and prepare for certification in medical management.

Survey results and anecdotal reports substantiate the inclusion of incentive compensation as part of the physician executive's salary, consistent with incentive compensation's growth as part of the senior executive team's compensation (Kirschman and Grebenschikoff 1997). Without adequate performance evaluation, incentive compensation will backfire.

Once in an organizational role, the physician manager should seek out mentoring and peer relationships. Clinicians routinely report the invaluable quality of having a trusted colleague with whom to share concerns and ideas, without violating confidential information. Within a health system, physician leadership groups are often established for periodic learning opportunities. The Internet and health system intranets offer unobtrusive opportunities to establish a learning community of peers. Professional development and advanced degree programs offer another potential resource.

Finally, the physician executive should be prepared for continued career transition and organizational change. Only 6 percent of the senior physician executives surveyed by Kirschman and Grebenschikoff (1997) expected their jobs to remain the same, and only 37 percent expected to remain in their current organizations with new duties. Role, functions, priorities, organizations, and environment are all very dynamic for contemporary physician executives and must be seriously considered.

Summary

This chapter has identified seven broad skill sets generally agreed upon for physician managers: clinical competence, including clinical board certification; interpersonal skills; personal management competence; quality management; computer literacy and information system skills; system thinking; and transformational leadership skills. Making the transition from clinician to physician manager may require substantial cognitive, attitudinal, emotional, and behavioral change, which will not be effective for every potential physician executive. The role of physician executive is itself dynamic, within the organization and from one organization to another. Nevertheless, a demand for physician managers has been established, and we expect more specific professional requirements to develop as the profession matures.

Acknowledgment

The author expresses her gratitude to Robert L. Brooks, M.D., and William G. Plavcan, M.D., for their very helpful comments on an earlier version of her chapter.

References

Belenky, M, B. Clinchy, and N. Goldberger. 1986. *Women's Ways of Knowing: The Development of Self, Voice, and Mind.* New York: Basic Books.

Bridges, W. 1980. *Transitions: Making Sense of Life's Changes.* Reading, MA: Addison-Wesley Publishing Company.

Burns, J. 1978. *Leadership.* New York: Harper & Row.

Cahoone, L. 1996. *From Modernism to Postmodernism: An Anthology.* Cambridge, MA: Blackwell Publishers.

Cervero, R. 1981. "A Factor Analytic Study of Physicians' Reasons for Participating in Continuing Education." *Journal of Medical Education* 56 (1): 29–34.

Comprehensive Accreditation Manual for Hospitals. 1997. Oakbrook Terrace, IL: Joint Commission on the Accreditation of Healthcare Organizations.

Covello, V. 1991. *Risk Comparisons and Risk Communication.* Boston, MA: Kluwer Academic Publishers.

Covey, S. 1989. *The Seven Habits of Highly Effective People.* New York: Simon and Shuster, Inc.

Cummings, K. 1988. "Why Some Managers Fail." *Physician Executive* 14 (4): 6–8.

Gill, S. 1977. "An Exploration of Physician Leadership Roles and Related Competencies across Health Care Market Stages." Unpublished dissertation proposal.

———. 1997. "Physician Leadership Development in Advanced Health Care Markets." Working manuscript. Westmont, IL: Physician Management Resources, Inc.

Grebenschikoff, J. 1995. "The Changing Role of Physician Executives." *Physician Executive* 21 (9): 7–12.

Hudson, F. 1991. *The Adult Years: Mastering the Art of Self-Renewal.* San Francisco, CA: Jossey-Bass Publishers.

Jung, C. 1971. *Psychological Types,* a revision by R.F.C. Hull of the translation by H. G. Baynes. Princeton, NJ: Princeton University Press.

Kindig, D. 1997. "Do Physician Executives Make a Difference?" *Frontiers of Health Services Management* 13 (3): 38–42.

Kindig, D., and A. Kovner. 1992. *The Role of the Physician Executive: Cases and Commentary.* Chicago: Health Administration Press.

Kirschman, D. 1996. "Physician Executives Share Insights." *Physician Executive* 22 (9): 30–33.

Kirschman, D., and J. Grebenschikoff. 1997. *Physician Executive Compensation Report: A 1995–96 Survey and Ten-Year Trends.* Tampa, FL: Physician Executive Management Center.

Kongstvedt, P. 1995. *Essentials of Managed Health Care.* Gaithersburg, MD: Aspen Publishing, Inc.

Kotter, J. 1990. *A Force for Change: How Leadership Differs from Management.* New York: Free Press.

———. 1996. *Leading Change.* Boston, MA: Harvard Business School Press.

Kouzes, J., and B. Posner. 1988. *The Leadership Challenge: How to Get Extraordinary Things Done in Organizations.* San Francisco: Jossey-Bass Publishers.

———. 1993. *Credibility: How Leaders Gain and Lose It, Why People Demand It.* San Francisco: Jossey-Bass Publishers.

LeTourneau, B., and W. Curry. 1997. "Physicians as Executives: Boon or Boondoggle?" *Frontiers of Health Services Management* 13 (3): 3–25.

Linney, G., and B. Linney. 1992. *Medical Directors: What Why, How.* Tampa, FL: American College of Physician Executives.

Lloyd, J. 1994. "What Kind of Leaders Will Be Successful?" *Physician Executive* 20 (3): 8–11.

McCall, M. 1990. "Why Physician Managers Fail—Part I." *Physician Executive* 16 (3): 6–10.

McWhinney, W. 1993. *Of Paradigms and System Theories.* Santa Barbara, CA: Fielding Institute.

Nadler, D., R. Shaw, and A. Walton. 1995. *Discontinuous Change: Leading Organizational Transformation.* San Francisco: Jossey-Bass Publishers.

Porter, M. 1980. *Competitive Strategy: Techniques for Analyzing Industries and Competitors.* New York: Free Press.

Senge, P. 1990. *The Fifth Discipline: The Art and Practice of the Learning Organization.* New York: Doubleday.

Senge, P., C. Roberts, and R. Ross. 1994. *The Fifth Discipline Field Book; Strategies and Tools for Building a Learning Organization.* New York: Doubleday.

Shortell, S., R. Gillies, D. Anderson, K. Erickson, and J. Mitchell. 1996. *Remaking Health Care in America: Building Organized Delivery Systems.* San Francisco: Jossey-Bass Publishers.

Shull, F., et al. 1970. *Organizational Decision Making.* New York: McGraw Hill.

Silbiger, S. 1993. *The Ten-Day MBA: A Step by Step Guide to Mastering the Skills Taught in America's Top Business Schools.* New York: Morrow.

Striano, J. 1988. *Future Terrific: Planning Change in Mid-Life.* Santa Barbara, CA: Professional Press.

Totten, M., and J. Orlikoff. 1996. *Medical Leadership in Outstanding Organizations: Borgess Health Alliance.* La Jolla, CA.: Medical Staff Leadership Forum of the Governance Institute.

Vanvoorhees, C., et al. 1988. "Learning Styles and Continuing Medical Education." *Journal of Continuing Education in the Health Professions* 8 (4): 257–65.

Veloski, J., et al. 1996. "Medical Student Education in Managed Care Settings beyond HMOs." *Journal of the American Medical Association* 276 (9): 667–727.

Wheatley, M. 1992. *Learning and the New Science: About Organization from an Orderly Universe.* San Francisco: Barrett-Kohler.

Williams, S., and C. Ewell. 1996. "Medical Staff Leadership: A National Panel Study." *Health Care Management Review* 21 (2): 29–37.

Plotting a Course of Growth

Mark A. Doyne

S O THIS is the situation: The newly hired physician executive (PE) has been brought on board and is now part of the senior management team. This may be the PE's first foray into management; the new job may be part or full time. Or he or she may have held one or more prior management positions. The hiring organization also may be establishing its first PE role; perhaps it is expanding or altering the initial position.

For the newly hired PE, it is critically important to understand the background and historical perspective of the PE position being assumed. If it is a new position, why has it been established and what are the critical expectations? If the role has been reengineered, again, why? Ideally, some detailed questioning and research has been performed before the position was accepted. And what of the politics? Where are the land mines? Who are the influence agents, and with whom does the PE need to partner to achieve success? Certainly the PE cannot and will not ascertain all the answers to these and other questions ahead of time, but these elements are important and should be explored. If someone has already served in the role being accepted, an honest and open conversation with that person can provide invaluable insight.

Here We Go

By now, the PE should know—at least somewhat—how he or she fits into the organizational chart. Many PEs report directly to the chief executive officer, especially in single hospitals or in smaller healthcare organizations. More and more, however, with the profusion of mergers, alliances, and acquisitions, the new PE may report to a more senior PE or to a vice president or senior vice president of operations. Each of these reporting relationships carries certain implications, challenges, and opportunities. Perhaps the most important aspect of the position for the new PE to understand is the organization's corporate culture; ideally this homework took place before starting the job. The corporate culture "fit" is, in my opinion, the most crucial factor in determining whether any employee will thrive or perpetually struggle. What is the corporate culture? Simply put, it is the set of core values and beliefs that determine organizational behavior; they are truly the "soul" of the organization. If the new PE finds him- or herself in corporate cultural misfit or misalignment, failure and misery (on both sides) will almost certainly ensue. If there is corporate cultural harmony, the new partners will be able to overcome almost any obstacles and challenges.

It is important that the reporting relationship be crystal clear. (Believe it or not, it sometimes is not!) A written job description must be mutually agreed upon. If the job description is already in place, it must be agreeable to the PE even if it is not mutually agreed to. The job description breaks down the larger roles and responsibilities and the specific tasks associated with each area. An example of a large area of responsibility might be "is responsible for the overall quality of care of ABC organization." Associated tasks could include developing standards of care or ensuring high-quality care by working with the medical staff through the organization's bylaws or medical policies and procedures.

Equally important is an explicit mutual understanding of exactly how the PE's job performance will be measured. I believe it is best, whenever possible, to make performance evaluation as objective as possible. Most performance indicators can be measured or quantified in some way; performance targets and timelines should be agreed on and put in place. The PE should also demand at least quarterly performance reviews with his or her superior to help ensure that the PE is "tracking." A common cause of failure is misunderstanding between employee and supervisor with respect to job priorities and how the employee's time should be spent. The best way to avoid this disconnection is through frequent communication about short- and long-term job-related goals.

The role of the PE has evolved over the past 25 years. Previously, the primary reason to have any kind of physician on the management team was as a caretaker or liaison. No more! Each of us is now challenged to add value to his or her organization. We do this through specific competencies that enable the organization to achieve goals previously unattainable. An example might be in the area of information systems and medical data management. Perhaps a better descriptor might be medical informatics. Successful deployment, analysis, and application of data by a skilled PE can enhance not only clinical outcomes but also the bottom line. The PE must, therefore, chart a course of professional education and growth so as to become a positive change agent for his or her organization. A repertoire of core competencies must be developed (see page 103). For the clinician, these competencies may parallel learning surgical skills, how to perform a history and physical, or how to write admission orders. Simply being a good clinician brings absolutely no guarantees of success in the new world of medical management.

Synergistic Growth

What should exist is a partnership between the new PE and the hiring organization. Figure 6.1 shows that each has needs that coincide and others that do not. A visual audit can now provide specific direction for the PE regarding competencies that are needed to address immediate organizational needs. If an organizational priority is to improve clinical quality, the PE will need to bring data management and medical informatics skills to the management table. If this is a weakness or void in the PE's armamentarium, the PE must do whatever is necessary to become skilled in the area or to hire people with such skills. Another approach, this time from the PE's perspective, would be to recognize certain management gaps or relative weaknesses and ask management for an opportunity to work in these areas. For instance, if the PE aspires to move toward the operational side of the organization, he or she should ask for some line management responsibilities. In addition, a mentor, internal or external, can be of great value to the PE.

Together, the PE and the hiring organization should plot a course of growth for the PE that is consistent with the needs of both parties. Organizational priorities will steer the early course; however, as organizational needs evolve and as the PE gains stature, the focus will almost certainly change. For instance, as the PE is assigned greater responsibilities, advanced training in leadership will surely be advantageous. Perhaps honing negotiation or strategic planning skills or gaining advanced training in finance and accounting will be of value to the PE. These and other needs will arise naturally as the career of the PE evolves within the organization. The time and resources to achieve mutual success should be hammered out along the way.

Figure 6.1   Competencies and Needs

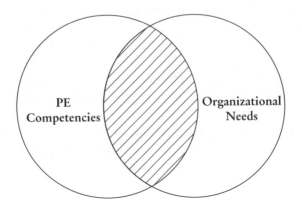

Adding Value

Let's take a broad look at the healthcare industry. The pace of change is quickening and shows no signs of slowing down. Expansion and mergers and acquisitions are an everyday occurrence. Payors are becoming providers, and providers are becoming payors. Physicians are realigning and reorganizing in myriad permutations. While physician management service organizations are emerging and growing, the jury seems to be still out on whether these MSOs really add value. There is a move afoot for physicians to "take back medicine." Hospital (systems) and physicians are partnering with varied success. The line between for-profit and not-for-profit organizations is blurring. Many of the old rules have gone out the window!

But from chaos generally emerges order. And of what will that order consist? In healthcare, I believe it will consist of cost-effective, high-quality care. Those who can deliver on this promise will thrive, while others will fall by the wayside. Virtually all aspects of quality can be quantified or measured. To patients, quality means that they were seen on time, that their physician spent enough time with them, that their questions were answered, and that they felt that their physicians really cared about them. To employers or health plan administrators, quality means access and availability of healthcare services, timely communication back to them, and provision of value for their healthcare dollar. Clinicians generally think of quality in more scientific terms, such as a percentage of successful treatment outcomes, complication rates, and mortality rates, to name a few.

Because every constituency appears to have its own definition of quality, does this lead to schizophrenia on the part of providers? I don't think so, and this is exactly where the PE can make a difference and add value in his or her organization. I believe that the best way to achieve cost-effective care is by providing "best care." If the provider does the right thing, at the right time, in the right way, the result is almost always not only a higher quality of care but lower cost! The higher quality of things done right should be obvious; the lower costs come from avoiding the necessity to make corrections or to compensate for errors. Many physicians feel that higher quality equals higher cost; however, the enlightened PE can demonstrate that this is not the case. And again, this belief can be measured and validated.

So what are some of the skills, the core competencies that the new PE needs to master? Following is a list of some of the most important:

- organization dynamics and behavior;
- managing change;
- communication skills;
- healthcare finance and accounting;
- healthcare law;
- medical ethics;
- managed care; and
- leadership skills.

Sooner or later, all of these skills, and many more, will need to be mastered by the successful PE. My personal advice for the PE who is 40 years old or less would be to get involved with the American College of Physician Executives—but also to obtain an advanced degree such as an M.B.A., an M.H.A., or a master's degree in medical management. The competition is really heating up!

A Dose of Reality

The discussion above obviously makes the assumption that the PE and the hiring organization "get married and live happily ever after." We all know that this is often, maybe usually, not the case. There are myriad reasons for this result, ranging from organizational changes and evolution to the needs and growth of the PE. This is not necessarily "bad" for either party. That said, the basic approach that has been outlined above represents a good road for both the hiring organization and the PE to travel; even if the two should part ways, other partners will emerge. Fundamental mutual commitment speaks volumes and is the best way to achieve mutual success.

Building Trust in Contentious Times

Kenneth C. Cummings

TRUST IS a defining ingredient in all human relationships. Whether the trust level is zero or total, it defines exactly how the persons involved will view and deal with one another. And, although trust is essentially a one-on-one commodity, it has group overtones, especially in organizations. How individuals relate one-on-one combines within an organization to determine how individuals and groups of individuals view the trust element of their relationship to the organization.

Although trust is an ever-present factor in human relationships, it is more significant in times of change, especially rapid change. When we are able to accommodate and adapt to change in reasonable time, trust is important, but timing is a bit less critical. We can anticipate the change and preadjust for its impact. We still have to trust that the actions of others will not be significantly dissonant from our own, but the consequences of dissonance are not yet unacceptable. We have the time to adjust. Trust is easier, because outcomes arrive at a more leisurely pace.

But when the speed of change outpaces our ability to respond and adjust in real time, we simply have to trust that we can survive long enough to make adjustments and deal with the change. We have to trust that individuals relaying information on the change are dealing with us openly and honestly, that there are no hidden agendas that will make it difficult to deal with the current wave of change and perhaps impossible to deal with subsequent waves.

In times of change, then, trust is a coping mechanism that allows us simply to accept certain elements of change so that we can concentrate on those elements that are most likely to help us adapt to and personally incorporate the change. How each of us copes and how we cope in groups will determine how the organizations we serve deal with change. It will be my contention in this chapter that the building of trust at all levels of the organization is critical to the organization's response to change. The construction will be more important at some levels than others, but levels of trust will be required everywhere.

The Various Aspects of Trust in Relationships

Let us begin with some thoughts on trust in one-on-one interpersonal relationships. References vary in wording, but a good working definition of trust can be defined as acknowledgment of the presence of and reliance upon:

Integrity. Each party to a relationship must believe that the other tells the truth, the whole truth, and nothing but the truth.

Capability. Each party to a relationship must believe that the other parties are capable of fulfilling their parts of the task upon which the relationship is based.

Character. Each party to a relationship must believe that other parties are committed to the relationship, that they will perform as expected even when no one is looking or monitoring their behavior.

All of these elements must be present in a relationship, or trust is not possible. The level of trust will depend on the degree to which each of the elements is present. For example, someone may have high integrity and outstanding character but be capable of accomplishing only part of the task at hand. As long as the person stayed within his or her capabilities, trust would remain high. However, trust would suffer if the person assumed or was expected to assume tasks outside his or her competence. The intensity of the trust developed in a relationship is proportional to the level of trust required (for example, trusting someone with a dime to buy you a cup of coffee versus trusting someone to watch over your child). The elements function synergistically to enhance mutual respect. Respect in a relationship is really little more than an acknowledgment by participants that their partners are trustworthy. When all of the elements are present and trust is ensured, very positive outcomes are made possible.

The three elements of trust translate into a set of operating characteristics for the trusting relationship. Again, all of these characteristics must be present or the relationship will be suboptimal. And when a relationship fails, its expected outcomes remain unattained. This latter point is most important in personal relationships, but it also applies to organizational relationships. Times of great change require tight and very dependent relationships. In the absence of trust, such relationships are highly unlikely to form, or, if they form, to survive long. The participants will soon be acting only in their own best interests and the effort will sink. My list of the characteristics of a trusting relationship is:

- willingness to share risk;
- willingness to cooperate;
- willingness to consider other views as validation of the "worthwhileness" of other individuals;
- initial acceptance of factuality or legitimacy of information, data, philosophy, thesis of other individuals;
- belief that other individuals will act in mutual best interest;
- belief in honesty of other parties;
- openness of communication;
- absence of "hidden agendas"; and
- willingness to relinquish control, authority, or primary role.

To understand the nature of trust in a relationship, it is also necessary to understand the conditions for the absence of or diminution of trust. When trust is lacking or minimal, heavy emphasis is usually placed on contracts or other legal documents defining the parameters of the relationship. Less reliance is placed on mutual trust to complete the task. But this is a shaky arrangement, especially in times of great change. Because the partners to the relationship are not linked by trust, the fragile balance that keeps them tied to the relationship is easily upset. If the partners in a group medical practice are linked only by the partnership agreement and not by any sense of trust in mutual commitment to the practice, "predators" are much more likely to find a path to acquiring the practice by playing on the absence of group trust and, thus, cohesion.

Regardless of the type of relationship, the basic elements of trust are the same. The emphasis on and relative importance of the elements will vary, but all the elements must be in place. This is particularly true in business relationships, where the extent or depth of trust required, the organizational culture, and personal and organizational goals greatly influence the characteristics of the relationship.

Of course, groups of people, companies, and corporations are still made up of and represented by individuals. While trust among individuals in these settings is critically important, because companies and corporations, individuals in the aggregate, are functional parts of the trust relationship, a new element of depersonalization is added to the equation. Each party to the corporate relationship must develop an independent trust relationship with the company as a whole, and this is considerably more difficult with a depersonalized company or corporation.

Further, the company or corporation may "see" the individual differently than would an individual. This suggests that organizational leaders may evaluate individuals and relationships differently, depending on whether they are evaluating from their point of view or from that of the corporation. To develop strong trusting relationships involving corporations, the above must be acknowledged and addressed and any dissonance minimized. In developing these relationships, it is important to put "faces" on each of the trust-relationship parties. In fact, the use of certain kinds of language in the relationship are a clear indication that trust has been replaced by either submission or dictation. When a subordinate shrugs in response to being asked to do something and says that it's the company's way, or when a superior, in response to subordinates' resistance to a directive, falls back on "That's the company's policy," trust has been replaced by fear and subservience on the subordinate's part and by dependence on position on the part of the superior. Neither party is well-positioned to deal with change. Rather than assessing the status quo, both will be inclined to resist any movement from it.

General Guidelines on Developing Trust in Relationships

Trust in organizational relationships is built one pair at a time. In the perfect world, each participant in the organization would trust all other parties at all times. This is not a perfect world, so there will be flaws in relationships. There will be zero or limited trust between some participants at all times and in particular instances. Where trust is zero, the relationship cannot long endure. Where it is limited, the organization's ability to deal effectively with change will be severely compromised. So, how can trust be developed?

- **Understand who you are, what your intentions are, and what goals you hope to achieve.** To understand how we relate with others, we must have a firm grasp of ourselves, and such understanding requires a conscious effort. After you have an understanding of yourself, make a major effort to do the same for the other "partners" in the relationship, whether they are employees, managers, vice presidents, or associates in business. It is rarely possible to know others as well as we should know ourselves, but even an imperfect assessment of others is better than no assessment at all.

- **Focus on individuals.** Trust in organizations is ultimately based on trust in individuals and on their capability to influence the organization. Focusing on individuals will also tend to insulate you from an expectation of victimization by the actions and opinions of others. The organization has no opinions, and actions cannot be taken by the organization. You and your partners in the organizational relationship must do both. To so do effectively and move the organization forward, you must trust one another.

- **Expand communication.** In the absence of communication on an issue in a relationship, we are inclined to suspect the worst, or at least some negative outcome.

- **Don't underestimate the importance of the process.** It becomes the outcome. The development of trust is a slow process. Through continual testing and the accretion of evidence that trust is well placed, we arrive at a trusting relationship.

- **Combat arrogance at all levels.** Commonly, this is subtly and perhaps subconsciously related to position or title. Persons higher in the hierarchy presume an additional importance for their views and actions, and those below them acquiesce to the presumption. All too frequently, inadequate views are thus elevated and good ones are lost. When the outcome, predictably, is disastrous, trust is lost. Subordinates wonder how the leader could have taken them to such a result; the leader wonders why he was allowed to travel such a pitted road.

- **Be willing to take risks in the relationship by trusting first.** A trusting relationship cannot be developed if no one takes the first step. Few would want to be a participant at any time in an organization in which no one was willing to take this risk. In stressful times—and change is always stressful—the paralyzed organization is likely to be washed away by the first wave.

- **Make the sharing of information a part of your communication.** Information *is* power, and, when you share it, you share power. This greatly facilitates the development of trust, but it can seem very threatening to those in powerful positions or having powerful titles. The leader must understand that failure to share information broadly reflects the arrogance described in an earlier point. The leader may feel comforted by knowing what others do not, but the others will be hard pressed to trust such a leader, let alone give their best to the organization.

- **Move from reliance on positional power to reliance on relational power.** In a trusting relationship, the parties must believe that their partners are committed to the good of the relationship and its goals, not solely to personal goals.

- **Look for something to respect in the other party.** If you respect a person's technical competence, you are prepared to trust his or her technical decisions and actions. That makes it easier to trust an action or decision outside the technical area.

- **Be trustworthy yourself.** Signal your trustworthiness when you have confidence in it.
- **Look for commonality of interests and goals and actively amalgamate them.** Determine where you share views and goal paths with others and concentrate on these common areas. When you and others can know, and trust, in positions in limited areas, it makes it easier to build trust in areas of divergence.
- **Have patience.** Trust evolves over time, but its evolution can be managed. Strategize on priorities to develop early trust.
- **Hold a stable vision.** When people are in the trust-building process, they will be focused and very sensitive to variations in message, actions, and words. They will be looking for consistency from you. Provide it. But do not take this as an admonition to eschew change. If the variations take a logical course, they will still be viewed as consistent with your vision.
- **Avoid premature conclusions regarding other persons' motivation or capability of being trusted.** It is prudent, of course, to be alert, but prejudgments can stifle trust before it has a chance to develop.
- **Avoid words, facial expressions, gestures, and other body language that suggests suspicion, another agenda, or lack of interest.** The signal is that you are not trusting, not interested in trusting, or not prepared to be trusting or trusted.
- **Avoid manner of dress or actions that would suggest that your values and philosophies are significantly aberrant.** An organization, even a part of an organization, has "cultural" leanings and attitudes that can cause rejection of persons who differ significantly in appearance or actions from cultural norms. Organizations can change culturally, of course, but the members of the organization will be more willing to accommodate such change after a new member has demonstrated attachment to the organization's existing culture.

Trust in Healthcare

The U.S. healthcare system is unique in the extent to which trust is required for daily operations. Trust is so essential because the chances of error are great and because the cost of errors is so enormously high. The degree to which each of the constituent groups trusts others is directly related to the educational and cultural backgrounds, the philosophies, the experiences, the biases, and the goals of the members of the group.

Owners

From a physician's point of view, it seems alien to consider provision of healthcare in terms of ownership, but the evolution of the healthcare environment in terms of managed care and integrated healthcare delivery systems has spotlighted these stakeholders. Each of the owner groups has its own definitions of terms and rationales for its positions. Stockholders see themselves as providing capital for the development of the industry and, obviously, expect an economic return on their investments. Corporate executives see healthcare as a business. Insurance companies and managed care organizations see themselves as owning "covered lives," and, indeed, from market and legal points of view, these "covered lives" do have economic value. Physicians commonly believe that they "own" their relationships with patients; some hospitals and insurers seem to agree, because dollars are being paid for these relationships. The IRS has another opinion. Businesses and federal and state governments sometimes behave as though they own their employees', veterans', and Medicare and Medicaid patients' medical lives.

The obvious point is that there are many actual and self-perceived "owners" within our changing healthcare environment, and they have divergent—sometimes wildly divergent—views of what the healthcare system is and where it should be going. All of them are locked in relationships with multiple sets of subrelationships. The parameters of trust in many of these relationships are confirmed in contractual terms to minimize the actual trust needed to make the relationships functional. Heightened stress in the relationship and the necessity of a broader, deeper trust become evident when the partners in the relationship have dissimilar goals, approaches, or philosophies.

Trustees or Board Members

Trustees of healthcare organizations bring a variety of experiences, education, expertise, biases, and interpersonal relationships to the board. Significant trust in a community hospital board of trustees is difficult to develop, particularly for individuals with a significant stake in the board's actions. Further, because the board of trustees has no direct relationship with those influenced by its actions, it is easy for trustees to function impersonally, which easily damages trust. There are ways to facilitate relationships with boards:

- Each side must be knowledgeable about the issues of concern. This means that the effort to educate the other side must be taken seriously.
- Each side must affirm the legitimacy of the others' positions.
- Each side must strive for predictability in actions.
- Each side must behave with integrity and trustworthiness. Such behavior leads to mutual respect, which is essential if progress is to be made and peace is to exist.

Administrators

The profound level of stress found in today's changing hospitals is largely responsible for hospital management appearing "bureaucratic" and less sensitive to physicians. Under pressure, most of us rest more heavily on rules and policies, particularly when those with "power" make demands we consider inappropriate. Over the years, the large majority of healthcare management professionals I have observed and worked with have been dedicated, intelligent, and solid professionals. Hospital boards and physicians have not given them the credit and acclaim they deserve.

Nurses

Trust between doctors and nurses is not fundamentally different from that found between others; it is just that the implications of the level of trust for both professionals and for the patient are so great. Suffice it to say that the nurse will trust when he or she observes the physician performing duties for patients, over time, in an excellent manner, while treating nurses and other workers as professionals and with dignity. The physician expects the nurse to carry out clinical orders exactly, to ensure the patient is being well cared for, to communicate the information the physician needs when a change occurs, and to give the physician due respect. There are so many opportunities to destroy trust, it is a wonder that any exists between physicians and nurses. But it does, because most doctors and most nurses are consummate professionals.

Physicians

Physicians' attitudes toward change, generally in the healthcare field and specifically within the medical profession, depend to a large degree on their age grouping. More senior physicians are less willing, sometimes even unwilling, to change. They are holding on for the salvation of retirement. Physicians currently in midcareer may be willing to change, but most are only grudgingly willing to change and then only minimally to meet new healthcare realities. Physicians in the early stages of their careers have very different values. They are usually willing and eager to accept significant change, as long as their basic patient care philosophy is not breached.

A major reason that so many physicians are agitated, anxious, depressed, and somewhat bitter is that they committed to a profession that offered a predictable and stable set of expectations in exchange for an extended and brutal training period and long hours of work and responsibility. Unfortunately, after struggling to midcareer and to a full practice, they find the rules have been changed, and the new expectations are not nearly so appealing. To say that physicians are having difficulties trusting the system or any of its representatives is an extreme understatement.

Even for most professionals in the healthcare industry, current economic and clinical healthcare realities are so complex and obscure that they have a superficial, limited understanding. So many players. Such important issues. Can anyone be trusted?

Building Trust at the Operational Level

As challenging as it is to define and dissect relational trust in abstract and philosophical terms adequately, this process pales in comparison to the challenge of actively managing the element of trust in the hourly performance of our roles in the current healthcare environment. It is a mind-stretching exercise to consider the differences in appearance of relational trust at "100,000 feet" versus at "ground level." At first, the two views bear little resemblance, but, upon contemplation, we begin to see the abstract elements of trust through their presence or absence in these everyday circumstances.

What follows is an effort to describe and briefly discuss how trust or its absence presents itself in our daily professional lives, in the context of dramatically differing roles and perspectives.

The Healthcare Workplace

As emphasized previously, trust begins, lives, and dies in the relationships of individuals. Each individual or group has its own cultural, educational, and experiential biases. Each speaks a unique form of "language," derived from its professional preparation and modified by its relational and other experiences and expectations.

CEO to Board of Trustees. In the performance of his or her role, the CEO must enjoy a level of trust with trustees that allows considerable latitude in decision making. Anything else is micromanagement and reflects that the trustees do not understand their role.

CEO to COO. If the chief operating officer (COO) does not trust the CEO's motives/capabilities, aggressive implementation of strategic and operational plans is jeopardized. If the CEO does not trust the motives or capabilities of the COO, insufficient support of multiple types will not be available to the COO and, again, implementation of strategic and operational plans is in grave jeopardy.

CEO to Physician Executive (PE). Because the PE serves as liaison between management and the organization's medical staff, trust is absolutely required for optimal success. Distrust in this relationship is unacceptable for multiple reasons, but most significantly because of the inherent difficulty and unpredictability of leading a medical staff.

COO to PE. Reporting relationships vary, but, commonly, both the PE and the COO report to the CEO. Higher level PEs commonly insist on reporting directly to the CEO, because service to physicians demand that level of access. Herein lies one of the central issues around which distrust grows between COOs and PEs. The COO, responsible for the operations, costs, and revenues of the organization, does not have the desired level of control of physicians because of their nonemployee, "agent" status. Estimates vary, but physicians probably direct the utilization of 70 to 80 percent of the organization's resources, resources not directly controlled by the COO. Additionally, medical staff physicians commonly have a perspective different from that of COO regarding various issues, including strategic ones, that are represented to the CEO by the PE. Further, the PE may disagree with the COO on operational decisions that adversely affect patient care. Unless managed with care, directness, and well-supported views, this relationship can lead to end runs, "politics," and terminal distrust.

PE to the Healthcare "System" Elements. In most systems, the advent of PEs is relatively recent, and, thus, the administrators of skilled nursing facilities, home health agencies, visiting nurse programs, rehabilitation and therapy programs, etc., do not know how to relate to the physician executive. Therefore, a trusting relationship must be established with each based on the principles previously discussed.

PE to Nurses. Nurses commonly have significant differences with physicians (and vice versa), and these differences become issues between the PE and the Director of Nursing. However they choose to deal with each another determines the level of trust attainable and the quality of resolution of the issues.

Nonphysician Executives and Managers to PE. In my experience, nonphysician managers require that the PE prove, over time, that he or she can be trusted and is a team member. The PE who represents the medical staff has tremendous influence on daily operations, resource utilization, service design, and budgets. If the PE reports directly to the CEO, increase that influence (code word for power) by a magnitude. Additionally, PEs are physicians, and common organizational cultural folklore has physicians pegged into modes of functioning that do not respect organizational structure or policies. Consequently, the PE must actively model his or her behaviors to invite trust.

Challenges Relating to Trust That Are Specific to the Physician Executive

Physicians who opt for the deep water of healthcare management experience the same trials, emotional and intellectual stretches, and deficits of knowledge and experience as do nonphysician managers. But because we are physicians and because one of our major direct roles is helping other physicians through the transitions noted previously, there are unique requirements, complexities, and challenges.

On professional matters, physicians share an unusual degree of trust, but this trust does not easily extend to relationships beyond the clinical. All of us, having gone through the same rigors of academic competition—physical, mental, and emotional challenges—automatically have significant understanding of the price our peers have paid and something about their personalities and the motivations that have sustained them. But realize that intense isolation evolves as a consequence of the above. This isolation, facilitating as it is in helping us focus on what we are about, sometimes limits our perspective and makes us distrustful of nonpeers and of other roles and things we do not understand. Additionally, physicians are taught to challenge everything for the good of the patient. This easily evolves into challenging everything, period. Therefore, it is predictable that physicians will challenge even one of their own if he or she assumes a role different than theirs that may significantly affect, modify, or limit their own prerogatives.

As mentioned above, relationships with nonphysician organizational leaders (vice presidents) have other dimensions, but, initially, the physician executive tends to be given credibility and trust only as a clinician. They await evidence of the physician's abilities as a manager. The physician manager can be very threatening to a nonphysician manager.

Because of the transitions occurring in the healthcare environment, each day the competitive "lines" for covered lives and relationships with sources of patients are being ever more definitely drawn, while physicians attempt to keep these same lines as poorly defined as possible to protect their options. Most community hospitals share medical staff members. Some of these physicians may/will have their principal office sites at competitors' facilities. These physicians may well have business and other relationships with competitor hospitals, physician groups, physician-hospital organizations (PHOs), or insurance companies. Yet their clinical appointment and medical staff privileges grant them legitimate and desired presence at your facility and in medical staff meetings. This becomes an immediate issue when, in pursuing a plan for trust development, medical staff relations require sharing of strategy in, for example, a medical staff development plan.

One additional example deserves inclusion because of its presence in the national healthcare marketplace—the PHO. The principal reason for creating a PHO is to provide a vehicle for physicians and hospitals to work together in a legal, economically beneficial way. In the current era of managed care, to compete successfully means to control costs. Recalling that physicians control a large portion of inpatient cost and much of office practice cost, one of the most critical success factors for a PHO is how the physician panel is constructed. Though there are multiple variations, for our purposes, we will define two: open panel, where any physician desiring inclusion will be admitted, and closed panel, where the panel is limited in various ways. Experience has confirmed that open panels do not allow for sufficient cost control, because nonselected physician practice patterns vary so greatly. A key ingredient in controlling cost and improving quality is decreasing clinical practice variation. The only way to do that is to select the physician panel using criteria that are based on economic outcomes related to clinical outcomes. Physicians have come to understand that a key to their professional survival is access to patients. Enter the dragon of exclusion—that is, no access to this incipient patient base. No wonder physicians in this situation become extremely angry, hostile, and impulsive, believing they have been wronged by the institution and by their colleagues, even though the exclusion was a result of the choices of their own practice.

It is absolutely true that the physician executive is tested every day regarding trust, and trying to be all things to all people may lead you to being nothing to many. It is not uncommon, particularly early in a new PE position, to see barriers erected by colleagues, which serve not only to protect their personal interests but also to challenge the PE's role.

In the following discussion, I would like to review briefly the attitudes, behaviors, and actions I have experienced that, cumulatively, move the new PE's relationship with the medical staff along quickest toward credibility, respect, and trust.

Integrity. With physicians' extreme level of distrust of the current healthcare environment, to fit the ill-informed judgments they may have constructed, they will be looking for additional evidence to support their beliefs. The PE can be the local representative for all that is wrong with the system or, alternatively, a rallying point for empowered physicians. The relationship will not be constructively productive for long without integrity.

Forthrightness. Physicians see themselves as having been "yanked around" so many times recently (by Medicare, Medicaid, insurers, peer review organizations, and so on *ad nauseum*) that they just want to hear open honesty.

Patience. For the PE, this requires a calm, disciplined, methodical approach to the seemingly constant interruptions and personal and professional issues that medical staff physicians, administrators, nurses, and a hundred more individuals have.

Communication. Physicians are hungry for the facts and for a rational, intellectual construct into which they will fit. In the absence of facts, physicians, like everyone else, will make the best of what little information they have.

Be alert. Problems, changes, and opportunities frequently appear rapidly. If you don't recognize them, you won't be able to minimize the damage, put a new spin on them, or embrace new options.

Be enthusiastic. Within limits, this too is a matter of discipline. The PE is in the necessary position of selling (representing positively) positions from the administration to the medical staff and vice versa. If you cannot generate some interest or enthusiasm, the wrong messages are sent and you become part of the problem rather than of the solution.

Work on building consensus. With consensus on a large enough scale, nearly anything is possible; without it, nearly nothing can be done. Consensus does not automatically mean among the entire medical staff, but rather among some of the "right" people, depending on the goal.

Develop your team-building skills. Those who can facilitate teamwork are significant organizational assets. Those who cannot will be led by someone else, at best; in most cases, they will simply be led to the door.

Solicit input and participation. When physicians are educated and are then invited into a circumstance in which they have a stake, participation will not be a problem. The difficulty at that point becomes one not of herding cats, but of herding lions.

Try not to take things personally. The difficulty is that, sometimes, they *are* personal. Recognize them as such and deal with them directly. Otherwise, remind yourself that you are not the center of the universe.

Finally, make sure that you are competent in the day-to-day technical aspects of a PE's professional life. You should be knowledgeable about credentialing, quality assurance/quality improvement, clinical organizational behavior, administrative and other relationships with physicians, healthcare law, healthcare economics, clinical outcomes, clinical protocol development, and strategic planning/marketing. No current PEs began with this level of expertise, but it is now becoming standard.

Being a physician executive is extremely challenging. It is a discipline like no other. Each of us can and must take the best of who we are, stifle some of our defensive habits, learn from our mistakes, and realize we are still physicians, bringing healing to our patients in different but critically important new ways. In the rapid state of transition that we are currently experiencing, motivating change while building trust is a tall order. But accomplishing both simultaneously is essential and can be done. It requires discipline. I have found that I must make a written list of elements of the required change, what the change will look like, and who must be involved. Then, while planning the process, I make every attempt to build upon relationships already developed or bring new people into the process to widen the sphere of trust within which my credibility and effectiveness reside.

Linking Physician and Nonphysician Management Roles in the Managed Care Era

Roger M. Battistella and Thomas P. Weil

THE QUESTION of whether physician and nonphysician roles can coexist harmoniously in the future managed care environment is problematic. It depends mainly on the circumstances in which linkage is pursued. If linkage is taken to refer to the presently established pattern in which physician managers deal predominantly with medical matters and report directly to nonphysician authority, this relationship has functioned reasonably well from the time professionally trained managers were first introduced into the health field and can be expected to continue to do so in situations minimally affected by the formation of large integrated health systems and related managed care developments. If, on the other hand, the reporting relationship is reversed so that physician managers are on top and nonphysician managers—habituated to being in charge—are relegated to secondary supportive positions, demotion of status could result in considerable acrimony and division regardless of how healthcare is organized and financed.

Recent growth in the number of physicians seeking managerial positions is expected to increase in the future, due to an oversupply of physicians; the expansion of integrated systems consisting of medical groups, hospitals, and insurers; and the growing complexity of health services delivery (Battistella and Weil 1996). Many physicians will be induced to seek satisfaction and rewards in administrative careers at a point in the evolution of managed care when market competition will impose difficult demands for more cost-effective and higher-quality health services, for both of which knowledge of clinical medicine confers strategic advantages.

More physicians occupying executive suite positions may stir anxiety among nonphysicians possessing master's degrees in health services administration (M.H.A.), who, along with those holding master's degrees in business administration (M.B.A.), have dominated most of the top management positions in the health sector throughout the past three decades. Whatever insecurity nonphysicians currently feel is bound to increase as the combined effects of hospital downsizing, integrated network development, and the spread of capitated health maintenance organizations (HMOs) result in fewer but larger-sized entities with a concomitant thinning of managerial layers and a shrinkage of executive openings (Battistella and Weil 1996).

Aspiring physician executives already perceive tension in their relationship with established nonphysician managers, as evidenced by allegations that an unofficial glass ceiling discriminates against them and curtails career advancement (LeTourneau and Curry 1997). Whether well founded or not, this outlook stems from a suspicion that many of today's top nonphysician managers feel that individuals with a medical degree are poorly suited by background and temperament to function effectively at the chief executive officer (CEO) level (Lazarus 1997). As stated by McCall and Clair (1990), this stereotype dissuades physicians from entering management, inasmuch as its credence expands with every known instance of physician-executive failure. The bias against physicians' rising to the management pinnacle is pervasive. It comes across implicitly, if not explicitly, most often in writings on organizational theory and management issues by academics affiliated with health administration programs (Shortell and Kaluzny 1997). While urging senior executives to recognize and accept physicians' expanding management roles, they generally assume that physician managers will remain subordinate to nonphysicians.

That more managerial positions of greater responsibility are now open to physicians provides little comfort, because these jobs continue to be medically centered, involving such conventional clinically oriented tasks as physician recruitment, credentialing, quality assurance, risk management, and utilization review, and to serve as a conduit for smoothing medical staff and CEO relations (LeTourneau and Curry 1997; Weissenstein 1996). With the exception of major academic medical centers and similar medical establishment bastions where professional values of peer eminence and collegial decision making continue to prevail, physicians usually are not entrusted with overall management and leadership responsibilities in healthcare organizations. But this may soon change as the result of managed care expansion and of the emergence of integrated health networks.

While tension in the physician manager and nonphysician manager relationship is predictable in the near future, we basically are optimistic that any discord can be satisfactorily contained and that competition for top management jobs will proceed as it does in other sectors of the economy, where the final selection of an executive depends on numerous factors. In the context of the health field, they consist primarily of these:

- What organizations must do to adapt to the critical social and economic trends disrupting and transforming traditional patterns of healthcare delivery—notably, aging of the population and slowing of economic growth that limits our nation's ability to continue to pay for health services on the basis of open-ended, fee-for-service arrangements. These powerful forces underlie the extensive influence of market forces and the sophisticated corporate strategies bearing on the organization, financing, and delivery of health services.

- The leadership qualities and capabilities sought by healthcare organizations in the various stages of their growth and by the dynamics of market-driven competitive elements affecting their survival and prosperity. More specifically, the challenges associated with the transition from freestanding facilities to complicated and powerful integrated delivery systems and from revenue maximization to cost containment, with the accompanying necessity to capitalize on new reimbursement formulas that reward performance instead of high costs. Above all else, the preferences of the organization's trustees and directors responsible for hiring and firing senior executives remain paramount.

Corporatization of Healthcare: Physician and Nonphysician Power Struggle Issues

Adaptation of the health sector to the social and economic dynamics propelling health services restructuring entails a radical shift of control over the practice of medicine. Organized medicine's prerogatives for self-governance and self-regulation are falling under critical scrutiny, and freedom and independence of clinical decision making no longer are accepted as sacrosanct. Deference to independent professional judgment, whereby physicians are free to do all they believe desirable for patients, is increasingly criticized as too expensive, imprecise, and arbitrary. Managed care's focus on scientifically grounded efficacy measures provides data for directing and quantifying physician performance in ways that, for the first time, enable management to add value by systematically controlling costs and raising quality (Morone 1997).

Also on the defensive are the not-for-profit practices that distinguish the health field from other economic activities. No longer can they be assumed inviolate. Traditional organizational and delivery modes are being severely tested by the infusion of aggressively competitive efficiency and cost-control methods formerly confined to business and industry (Relman 1992).

Bureaucratic principles and managerial powers long deemed antithetical to good patient care, along with commercial incentives that multiply conflict of interest problems intrinsic to medical practice, are in the ascendancy. The corrosive effects of these developments are accentuated by the degree to which physicians, whether because of an understandable instinct for self-survival or because of shallow opportunism, are seen to have bought into acquisitive and depersonalized marketplace practices. Their apparently growing indifference to public opinion from which their high status, generous income, and numerous privileges are derived is yet another disturbing development. If the indifference is real, it signals ingratitude and a willingness to abandon long-standing social obligations for unrestrained personal gain (Rodwin 1993).

If public policy endorsement of hitherto questionable competitive market behaviors finds justification as an expedient for evading entrenched health-sector opposition to long-delayed improvements in productivity and quality improvement, it simultaneously feeds apprehensions that commercialism will degrade healthcare to the level of a commodity and obscure its distinction as a public good (Kuttner 1997). Albeit initially slow to react to the dangers inherent in the corporatization of health services, the medical establishment has become more active in defending the virtues of clinical sovereignty and the special features of the physician-patient relationship historically differentiating medicine from other occupations (American Medical Association, Council on Ethical and Judicial Affairs Report 1995; Pellegrino 1986; McArthur and Moore 1997).

Why Physicians Should Be in Charge

Physicians' justification for their control over the delivery of health services is grounded in their assumed moral superiority and the conviction that healthcare is too important to be run as workaday commerce (Relman 1992; Rodwin 1993). The significance of healthcare to society is threefold: First, health is essential to individuals' integrity and their ability to carry out responsibilities in a way that other goods and services are not. Second, the potential for physicians to wield power over vulnerable patients distinguishes the physician-patient relationship from ordinary marketplace dealings. Third, the provision of healthcare is a manifestation of the worth society places on individual happiness and well-being (Freidson 1971; Moore 1970; Starr 1982).

Because of the special social purpose of healthcare and the complexities of medical practice at the point where services and patients meet, the public interest is best served by entrusting illness treatment to individuals whose behavior is guided, through careful selection and socialization in prolonged education and training, by a professional culture that obligates them to subordinate self-interest to the welfare of their patients.

Confidence in the benefits stemming from the alignment of professional public service values and patient advocacy explains why society has granted the medical profession special powers from antiquity to the present day (McArthur and Moore 1997; Freidson 1971; Moore 1970). The decision on whether to continue this arrangement has profound implications for minimizing the potentially large perverse clinical and social problems inherent in the self-interested behavior propelling the managed care movement. A danger of managed care is that its financial orientation may lead to too much management and too little care. The proclivities of commercially minded managed care enthusiasts are unhampered by the sort of ethical sensitivities that curb self-interested behavior among medical professionals. There is a much greater chance, therefore, that they will take advantage of asymmetries of information for personal profit, whereas physicians are more inclined to place care in front of profits— whether for themselves or for the benefit of management (McArthur and Moore 1997; Relman 1991; Fuchs 1997).

Therefore, the type of ownership and management of the corporate managed care entities displacing fee-for-service medicine is crucial to determining whether they will be run as investor-owned or public service enterprises—that is, whether the profits generated from greater efficiencies are returned to shareholders or are used to invest in social capital (Relman 1991; Nudelman and Andrews 1996). Investor-owned enterprises are prone to spend as little on healthcare as market conditions allow. To generate the rates of return on investment expected by shareholders, for-profit health companies invariably are inclined to want to control what physicians do clinically. Although fee-for-service reimbursement unquestionably contributes to overservicing, managed care incentives often pressure physicians to skimp on and withhold medically warranted procedures. This is why determining how to reward observance of financial objectives without compromising quality of patient care is one of the most complex challenges now confronting managed care plans.

For-profit, commercially owned plans typically spend 80 percent or less of every premium dollar received on hospital and medical care to satisfy investor demands and to cover administrative expenses (Jenkins 1996). This means that 10 to 12 percent of the premium dollar goes to shareholders rather than benefiting the community. Worse yet, the money typically goes out of healthcare altogether (Nudelman and Andrews 1996; Walters 1996). In comparison, the culture of not-for-profit plans favors the allocation of any surplus to more and better services and the subsidization of essential money-losing community services, such as indigent care, trauma centers, and teaching and research activities. Unlike for-profit organizations, in which the accountability of the board of directors is fixed on shareholders, the fiduciary responsibilities of not-for-profit trustees is much broader, involving patients, providers of care, purchasers, and the community. Therefore, not-for-profit healthcare organizations commonly spend 90 percent or more of premium revenues on health services (Nudelman and Andrews 1996; Walters 1996).

Benevolence of Physician Control Exaggerated

From a pro-market perspective, the medical profession's alleged moral superiority is greatly overrated. The reality of professional ethics is much less reassuring than the image. Changes in reimbursement incentives subjecting providers to financial risk coincides with a torrent of formerly shunned marketshare-grabbing advertising and marketing practices and with an upsurge of physician involvement in lucrative business arrangements that test the limits of conflict-of-interest prohibitions (Sparrow 1996). Core professional values are further enfeebled by the frequency and magnitude of the acquisitions and mergers rapidly reshaping the health sector to resemble more closely the world of big business, both in form and in the centrality commanded by financial and finance-related leadership skills. Suspicion that fraud and abuse may account for as much as one-tenth of all health spending has led the federal government to launch an intensive investigation into whether mainstream providers, including not-for-profit hospitals and elite medical centers, are engaging in misbilling and other illegal practices (Anders and McGinley 1997).

When viewed against the backdrop of these developments, self-proclamations of the medical profession's moral superiority appear sanctimonious, if not outright hypocritical. The profession's credibility is further strained by the failure of organized medicine to undertake improvements in cost and quality control that could have averted the proliferation of commercial and corporate practices now assailed as socially divisive and injurious to good patient care. Obstinacy on the medical profession's part in the face of nationally disruptive high rates of increase in health spending, together with its success in thwarting public efforts to achieve efficiencies through bureaucratic planning and regulatory means, gave policymakers the impetus to resort to market forces for generating greater cost and quality accountability in the provision of healthcare services (Battistella and Weil 1986).

It now is generally acknowledged that insulation from competitive forces allowed providers to run health services more for their own convenience than in the interests of patients and with a flagrant disregard for the problems high rates of increase in annual spending created for employers and the national economy. Evidence that much of the care given Americans is not only overly costly but medically questionable and unnecessary constituted a major stimulus for federal legislation supporting the diffusion of competitive-market values and practices throughout the health sector. Indeed, the volume of widespread waste constitutes the main source of the easy profits spurring the entry of private investors into the healthcare field. It is also a major justification for the push by federal and state governments to move Medicare and Medicaid recipients from fee-for-service into managed care (Battistella 1997).

Unlike the medical profession, competition is in concert with public policy. Market forces are compelling a long-wasteful sector of the economy to become more efficient and to reduce medically unjustifiable variations in clinical practice. Due principally to the unleashing of competition, an ossified collection of fragmented services, in which providers have wide latitude to determine their own compensation independent of the efficiency and quality of their work, is undergoing conversion into an economy-minded system of coordinated care. Market-based healthcare, as stated by Hasan (1996), is the best way available to guarantee high-quality care at affordable prices. The absence of price and quality accountability in the provider-friendly, noncompetitive alternative is, as shown by experience, an inducement for inefficiency and waste.

Public accountability, as noted by Williams and Torrens (1993), is arguably higher in publicly traded plans. Supervision by self-perpetuating boards of trustees and complacency emanating from seldom-questioned assumptions about their public trust status shields not-for-profit organizations from the intense scrutiny applied to for-profit organizations. Because of public disclosure requirements, it is frequently far easier to get financial and other performance data about for-profit enterprises than, for example, about a not-for-profit community hospital. Although studies generally indicate that not-for-profit hospitals as a group contribute more in the form of community benefits than do for-profit ones, considerable variation exists. A large number of them, according to a review of the evidence by Claxton and others (1997), receive tax exemptions that exceed the benefits they dispense. Failure to meet community benefit obligations, of course, is why some Blue Cross and Blue Shield plans no longer are tax-exempt. Conversion to for-profit status to gain entry to capital sources in equity markets that bypass the limitations of debt financing is yet another reason.

Although the managed care industry has made money while, despite a slow start, successfully bringing annual premium increases in employer-provided health insurance down to the lowest levels seen in decades and contributing much to curbing of health inflation, the national economy has benefited considerably as well (Anonymous 1997). The general public, regardless of insurance status, has also gained from market-driven improvements in consumer convenience. Instead of being required to travel to scattered delivery sites unavailable during evenings and weekends, disease-specific services, as described by Herzlinger (1997), are now becoming consolidated in more accessible locations and being provided at times more convenient to consumer schedules.

Whatever the magnitude of executive pay packages and investor returns, the market-provided rewards are justifiable in light of the larger returns to society in the above areas and in the spread of integrated delivery systems that permit the provision of seamless patient care along with improved monitoring and evaluation of expenditures and quality. To expect that the medical profession could have accomplished this voluntarily requires a leap of faith. It is unrealistic to expect that physicians would, if given the chance, proceed vigorously to enact changes inimical to their self-interest.

Any suggestion that medical ownership and control can insulate healthcare from the effects of new financial realities is comforting to contemplate but illusional. No less so than in other commercial pursuits, physician-directed enterprises functioning in a competitive environment, whether organized on a not-for-profit or for-profit basis, must contend with many of the same bottom-line pressures. In many instances they will have little choice but to raise consumer charges and cut payroll and money-losing services to avert financial insolvency. Economic forces are indifferent to good intentions. A professionally owned and operated not-for-profit plan may desire to return more of any efficiency savings to the community, but the possibility of doing so hinges on its acumen in meeting the test of competition and in resisting the self-interested demands of management and staff for more than their fair share of any fiscal surplus.

Corporate Leadership Opportunities Will Vary as Managed Care Evolves

However intellectually stimulating to contemplate in the abstract, ideological and political disagreements over who is best qualified to lead healthcare in the corporate era depend not only on the configuration of structural dynamics underlining the transformation of healthcare but also, more visibly, on the challenges organizations encounter as they move through different life-cycle stages (Griffith 1996). Accordingly, demand for nonphysician and physician leadership can be expected to vary as the focus of managed care moves from how to manage money, to how to manage physicians, and finally to how to raise the health status of populations. Broadly considered, five stages of development are identifiable, the first several of which already are far advanced in many parts of the country (Battistella and Weil 1996).

First Stage

Prior to the 1980s, managed care was somewhat of a curiosity that was not taken seriously by the health provider community. Although federal legislation in 1973 authorized and subsidized the development of health maintenance organizations (HMOs), overly restrictive features curtailed the growth and impact of managed care (Brown 1983). At this stage, managed care bore the strong influence of antecedents dating to the 1920s in which prepaid group practice was promulgated by socially minded health reformers as a way to make healthcare more accessible through a uniform monthly premium whereby the healthy subsidize the sick and to raise the quality of care through the power of group dynamics and managerial controls inherent in staff and group medical practice arrangements. Because of consumer dislike of features limiting their freedom of choice and the opposition of physicians to the bureaucratization of medical practice and intrusions into their clinical autonomy and financial independence, prepaid group practice was pretty much confined to the periphery of fee-for-service medicine. While most early managed care initiatives eventually floundered, a few survived and obtained considerable visibility and acclaim as progressive components of the contemporary managed care community—the Kaiser Permanente Medical Care Program, the Group Health Cooperative of Puget Sound, and the Health Insurance Plan of New York (Iglehart 1992).

Subsequent program design modifications and easing of restrictions stimulated managed care expansion and marketshare. Among the major factors contributing to enrollment growth were the infusion of private capital and more flexible benefits, which did much to increase the number and availability of managed care plans. In addition, managed care became more attractive among employees when they were free to choose between traditional indemnity insurance and different types of managed care options. Provisions for independent practice associations (IPAs), point-of-service plans (POSs), and discounted fee-for-service initiatives, notably preferred provider organizations (PPOs), accelerated physician and consumer acceptance by minimizing unpopular controls over clinical decision making and freedom of choice associated with more rigid staff- and group-model HMOs.

Managed care growth was further boosted by government's abandonment of cumbersome bureaucratic approaches to healthcare restructuring in favor of a free-market strategy, which sought to harness the power of provider self-interest for the attainment of public objectives (Battistella and Weil 1986; Krill 1995). Especially instrumental was the shift in Medicare hospital reimbursement from open-ended retrospective fee-for-service payment to a prospective payment system that for the first time put hospitals at risk through the assignment of fixed prices for each of a large number of diagnosis-related groups (DRGs). This action did much to legitimize the financial dynamic central to managed care and emboldened other purchasers to push providers in a similar direction. By instigating providers to compete against one another for marketshare and survival, financial insecurity has become a powerful force for modernizing an organizationally and managerially backward health sector, as manifested in ongoing progress in cost containment, clinical pathways and guidelines, and formation of integrated delivery systems. Although steadily increasing with time, the initial effects were inconspicuous.

First-stage managed care effects are minor, for the most part, and any opposition stirred tends to be fragmented and ineffectual. Among the more adventuresome health community members, curiosity prevails. Because the bulk of their revenues continue to come from unmanaged fee-for-service, providers' independence and financial security are not immediately endangered, and initially many accept part-time managed care contracts as a way to supplement income while accumulating valuable information about industry methods and trends. To establish a presence and lay the groundwork for future controls, managed care plans intrude lightly into the clinical field and physician practice styles remain largely unencumbered. Managed care has no need to be obtrusive at this time because of the many opportunities to make easy money. Profits are derived mainly through selective enrollment practices and sophisticated money management. Consequently, nonphysician managers possessing marketing and financial skills are highly prized by managed care plans in this phase. Physician managers, on the other hand, either are too few in number or lack credibility at this time to be a significant factor.

Within the provider community, the principal leadership challenge is to get hospitals and physicians to recognize and prepare for future managed care encroachment through the formulation of defensive measures aimed at increasing influence in the marketplace sufficient to retain control over the setting of reimbursement rates. Notwithstanding appeals to enlightened self-interest, disorganization prevails and power over pricing gravitates to major purchasers. As traditional fee-for-service income declines, dependence on managed care contracts increases.

Throughout this period, management leadership within the provider community remains dominated by nonphysicians heading acute-care facilities, whose status and power is a function of the fact that hospitals are better organized to deal with managed care challenges and have deeper financial pockets than physicians practicing solo or in small groups.

Second Stage

At this juncture, managed care penetration attains sufficient mass to make its presence felt. Somewhere in the range of a 25 percent managed care marketshare, the power equation begins to favor purchasers, and providers are compelled to become more accommodating. Managed care plans begin to question physician practice styles more assertively and insist on more detailed information for hospital admissions and lengths of stay. Providers start to experience cost pressures as volumes and operating margins decline. Surpluses in high-cost technologies and among medical specialists become less tenable, and, as a result, restructuring commences in earnest. Physicians able to obtain the support of colleagues in conceptualizing and implementing competitive responses that favor doctors command a high premium.

Apprehension of managed care's ability to disrupt harmonious hospital-physician relations induces hospital management to pursue new ways to secure physician loyalty—notably, through the purchase of physician practices and the formation of joint ventures in which physicians become employees or financial partners in medical staff organizations (MSOs). Many physicians resist these moves, however, out of suspicion that hospital management's true intention is to usurp their financial and clinical freedoms and thereby relegate them to a subservient position.

However, the likelihood of being left behind or crushed by the managed care juggernaut renders the status quo unacceptable.

Largely in the belief that the hospital needs them more than they need the hospital, physicians begin to combine into large single- and multispecialty groups capable of contracting directly with insurers and purchasers at prices below what hospitals can offer because of their higher overhead and operating costs. Separation from and competition with hospitals also provides long-range advantages. If reestablishment of ties become advisable, physician groups are positioned to bargain from strength and to extract better partnership terms. Business-oriented professional management expertise becomes more important for medical groups to enhance revenues and diminish costs.

Innovation in less-invasive tertiary services and advances in ambulatory surgery make it possible in principle for a large multispecialty group of 100 or so physicians to do nearly everything that is done in a 400-bed hospital today, except for the most complicated treatment procedures. Heightened awareness within acute facilities of their growing dependence on their medical staffs' cooperation motivates them to expand opportunities for physicians at senior management levels. Among hospitals enmeshed in zero-sum marketshare competition, the cooperation of physicians is crucial for maximizing charge-based patient referrals while simultaneously building infrastructure to compete in managed care markets.

Although more higher-paying and responsible managerial positions become available to physicians and they are assimilated more often into senior management teams, few of them succeed in crossing the general management divide. They continue to be regarded as high-level functionaries focusing on medical management issues and serving as bridges between CEOs and their medical peers.

Third Stage

Downsizing, cost cutting, and other efficiency measures intensify as provider clout in the marketplace continues to decline. Forward-looking providers who succeed in creating networks linking inpatient acute services with primary care and other components of the healthcare continuum grow in size and influence at the expense of confused and weaker rivals. Financially vulnerable hospitals close or convert to other service lines, and physicians outside the protective confines of networks either merge into countervailing groups or are forced to sell out or relocate to less-desirable geographic areas to practice their specialties. Remaining providers compensate for declining profit margins by expanding volume or by diversifying into less competitive healthcare arenas. Efficiency savings from reducing labor and other production costs boost short-term profits but dissipate as waste is eliminated.

HMOs previously able to dictate terms to their customers, because of a lack of competition in their market areas or the unavailability of good cost data, are no longer in a position to do so. An influx of new managed care plans, including provider-sponsored organizations, and steeper competition from formerly passive Blue Cross and Blue Shield plans creates a buyers' market. Assisted by the availability of more accurate cost data, purchasers and consumers become more assertive in their price and quality-of-care demands so that management of physician practice patterns receives closer attention, along with information systems enabling identification of cost-effective treatment methods. In this environment, employers' attempts to move employees from fee-for-service into managed care plans become easier and more successful.

Because of the priority given to price and quality competitiveness, physicians competent in using such management tools as clinical-fiscal performance methodologies, medical informatics, and continuous quality improvement are eagerly sought and welcomed into senior management teams. Some are catapulted into CEO positions and displace nonphysician executives who encounter difficulty in finding comparable positions at similar pay in other healthcare organizations. Entrepreneurial creativity and a willingness to assume risks become more highly prized top executive talents. Healthcare organizations increasingly look for CEOs who are comfortable with the uncertainties and ambiguities of forming alliances in a constantly changing environment. The ability to negotiate and broker deals and to resolve conflicts consequently commands greater attention.

Fourth Stage

Industry consolidation and the formation of powerful health alliances are a distinguishing feature at this point. Ever broader and better coordinated delivery systems emerge within and among inpatient, ambulatory care, and long-term care services in which participating organizations are contractually connected. Insurers and provider groups compete for marketplace supremacy.

Provider service organizations (PSOs) strive to capture savings accruing from the curtailment of waste by taking on the insurance function themselves and eliminating third party payors. Head-to-head competition with HMOs ensues. Capture of a larger share of the premium dollar becomes a major objective. Toward this end, many medical groups align themselves with physician practice management companies that have the know-how to run the business side of their practices and to negotiate successfully with purchasers of care. PSO momentum is assisted by a convergence of its interests with those of employers. Out of disenchantment with HMO inability or reluctance to reduce prices, employers anticipate savings from dealing with providers directly (Battistella 1997). The potential sums involved are substantial. Of the premium revenues collected, insurers commonly retain 15 to 20 percent for their own uses, including administrative expenses, retained earnings, and investor returns (Jenkins 1996; Cook 1997).

Employers find it advantageous to establish area business coalitions to enhance and expand their ability to extract price concessions and to gain better reporting of utilization and medical outcomes data from providers, but they are eventually disarmed by the taming of competition. The leverage accompanying consolidation enables providers to regain control of pricing and to minimize further incursions into clinical decision making, but it also creates conditions for increased public scrutiny and regulation. In addition to the disadvantages to business and industry of higher fringe benefit costs, consumers experience perceived, if not real, reductions in healthcare accessibility and quality as providers reacquire the capacity to run health services for their own advantage. Health organizations hoping to placate public criticism and to evade unwelcome restrictions are inclined to consider replacing the nonphysician CEO with physician leadership, particularly when the halo effect projected by a medical degree can smooth crucial negotiations with politicians and regulators who are in a position to affect the organization's financial soundness and freedom of action in the healthcare marketplace.

Increased pressure to link clinical and financial information to avoid potentially disastrous errors when assuming larger amounts of financial risk enhances the allure of a physician CEO. Those with a knowledge of both the business aspects of healthcare delivery and the intricacies of negotiating contracts with third party payors are especially attractive to providers and insurers. Good clinical and health information systems, moreover, become a competitive requisite. Access to vastly enlarged amounts of data on what happens to patients, in terms of specific treatments and outcomes, enables individuals adept in the uses of medical information technology to ascertain and enact more cost-effective disease management procedures. Price and quality competitiveness improves from the standardization now possible for the treatment of specific disorders, such as cancer, diabetes, asthma, and manic depression. It sharply reduces the waste and error resulting when individual physicians make ad hoc decisions based on differences in education, training, and personal experience. Statistical evidence of what works best for the least expenditure determines treatment, properly adjusted for differences in a patient's symptoms, medical history, and other relevant characteristics.

As clinical decision making becomes a more important component of a managed care plan's responsibilities, the need to maintain a good working relationship with physicians rises. Given their indispensability to the organization's ability to meet purchaser price and quality of care demands, the prospect of physician alienation is a source of considerable anxiety (Luke and Begun 1997; Zuckerman and Dowling 1997). How managerial authority is organized and implemented is an important determinant of the amount and severity of conflict possible when physicians are subjected to unfamiliar and distasteful forms of cost and quality accountability. The conflict potential also varies with timing, as resignation and acceptance gradually displace resistance among older fee-for-service–oriented physicians and as the number of younger physicians conditioned to accept managed care as a normal condition increases.

Throughout the transition from independent fee-for-service to the bureaucratic-corporate stage, the management of physicians may more closely approximate the herding of cats than any normal managerial activity. In recognition of the difficulty, enlightened management may prefer an indirect approach. Hospitals acquiring physician practices, for example, are likely to fail if they insist on running physician groups as if they were hospital units. Dissimilarities between the two favor treating the physician groups as a separate entity. Rather than risk escalation of tensions by taking direct responsibility for resolving such highly contentious issues as compensation and incentive policies and clinical performance measures, it is often wiser for central management to allow physicians to sort these elements and other thorny matters among themselves. Physicians habituated to clinical independence are more apt to resist nonphysician authority than are those entering managed care without any prior practice experience. In the interim, a gradualist approach provides a smoother transition to eventual full integration. Instead of forcing the issue, enlightened management will chose to concentrate initially on coordination of self-governing medical groups by monitoring and assessing performance in accordance with mutually agreeable criteria. Unity of purpose is obtainable through innovative organizational design, of which the following is illustrative.

Coordination of independent medical groups occurs by having them report to a physician-headed division of medical affairs occupying a line parallel with a separate division of business and administration headed by a nonphysician manager. To signify coequality, both divisions report directly to a CEO who is accountable in turn to a board of directors consisting of members jointly appointed by each division. Values and objectives are aligned through a system of shared authority. Equality of representation at the top facilitates compromise and cooperation. Inasmuch as neither side has a controlling voice, neither is able to ride roughshod over the other. As a practical matter, neither party is prone to propose anything totally unacceptable to the other. Within this framework, corporate-level responsibilities deal principally with the acquisition of capital, long-term planning, negotiation of contracts with healthcare buyers, and provision of administrative services to medical group practices. In return for these benefits, the medical groups allocate a percentage of their revenues to central administration and distribute the remainder as they see fit among their members, usually in a previously agreed upon manner (Shortell, Gillies, and Anderson 1994).

Fifth Stage

Coordinated, comprehensive delivery development culminates in the formation of vertically integrated networks. Because the ease of generating savings diminishes with shrinkage of surplus capacity, while societal demands for low prices and high quality remain steadfast, pressures mount for centralizing network services dispersed among multiple independent parties. Information system technology is insufficient to permit further improvements in cost and in quality controls demanded by purchasers and regulatory authorities.

Most of the easy savings are depleted at this stage. Uncompetitive facilities and programs have been forced to close, and surplus capacity has been eliminated throughout the system. Further productivity enhancements no longer can compensate for purchaser-imposed price and revenue reductions. Additional advances are best achieved in-house, where management can exercise tighter supervision and control and instill a peer culture of excellence through the power of group dynamics. Because the focus turns to quality improvement and value-added services, conditions favor the choice of a physician CEO. Once prospects for further productivity and efficiency improvements hit bottom, the focus of competition invariably shifts to quality and value additions to health services. The propensity of governing boards to prefer a physician CEO increases in recognition of the fact that corporations cannot practice medicine; only physicians are so empowered. Therefore, the ability to compete at this juncture becomes more physician-centered.

Megacorporate entities emerge, as contractually joined hospitals and multispecialty medical practices combine into fully integrated systems under a single management with annual revenues in the one-billion-dollar range. Within this giant corporate structure, the issue of leadership assumes increased importance. The ramifications of an amalgamation of physicians, hospitals, and capital resources under one corporate umbrella are enormous. Actuarial information and the capacity to connect financial and clinical data on a diagnosis- and provider-specific basis finally come together; and the possibilities for assessing the cost-effectiveness of alternative treatments and constructing scientifically sound outcome measures improve exponentially.

Concentration of executive authority, moreover, enables greater standardization of support activities and clinical proceedings through the control obtained over previously diffused and quasi-independent programs and personnel. Sizable reductions in unjustifiable variations in medical pricing and treatments within and across medical service areas are now feasible, and it becomes easier to tame medical inflation and to bring annual rates of increase in health spending into closer proximity to changes in the consumer price index.

Financial talent is no less significant at this point, but the marshaling and direction of human capital becomes paramount. This is the stage where managed care encompasses responsibility for the health of distinct populations in a more systematic way than was feasible under earlier competitive phases characterized by market uncertainty and high enrollment turnover. The juxtaposition of clinical medicine and social medicine objectives adds to the already formidable mix of key leadership requirements (McCall and Clair 1990; Smaha 1997).

Decision making becomes more complicated in this setting. As problems become less well defined and solutions surpass the capacity of single persons and departments, hierarchical management structures become inadequate and innovative group and team-based alternatives become more common. In searching for ways to tap the intellectual powers inherent in cooperative action, healthcare managers find it useful to look to other industries for suggestions. In this connection, there now is movement in business and industry to introduce self-organizing networks, known as *spider webs*, to make better use of the intellectual talent in the work force, which may be a preview of how authority will be distributed in large, complex managed care organizations (Quinn, Anderson, and Finkelstein 1996).

Typically, a spider's web swiftly combines the necessary talent from various areas and disciplines to solve a specific problem and then disbands once the task is completed. The multiplier effects of such interconnections are so great that even a handful of participants can leverage knowledge capabilities a hundred-fold or more. Command of advanced managerial techniques—and the ability to relinquish authority without losing control—is a prerequisite for anyone aspiring to a CEO position in the mature managed care stage, when society will insist that more and better quality care be made available to more people, including the poor and presently uninsured, without significant increases in spending.

Invincibility of Medical/Business Degree Combination

Expertise in both medicine and management is an uncommon but formidable combination that is sure to become more frequent, given that the future viability of managed care organizations hinges on an ability to assimilate medical and business perspectives and to treat adherents of each as coequals. Toward this end, holders of both degrees not only convey salient symbolic value but, more important, have the requisite knowledge and credibility for communicating it effectively to front-line clinical staff whose job performance ultimately determines the organization's success or failure. This is especially applicable to obtaining the support of physicians doing the work of daily patient care. Although professionals of all sorts accede more readily to the authority of peers, this attitude, according to Mitka (1994), is especially applicable to physicians.

As managed care plans move from loosely structured IPA models to more tightly structured group and staff models, the need for management to win and maintain physician cooperation and loyalty grows correspondingly. In addition to facilitating good management–medical staff relations and providing strategic insights into the complexities of clinical decision making, the medical/business degree combination is more conducive to containing harmful divisions among clinical and managerial interests. Among cost-conscious governing boards, there is the further allure of two-for-one savings in expensive executive salaries and the prospects of enhanced community standing for the organization because of widespread public respect for individuals of proven multiple abilities in widely different disciplines.

Medicine/Business Stress Factors

Ascent to the management pinnacle for physicians is a strenuous undertaking, involving steep opportunity costs and psychological discord. Mastery of requisite medical and managerial knowledge and skills entails long periods of study and practice, the opportunity costs of which are high in time and money. Successful entry into corporate life provides scant relief.

As described by Kaiser (1994), life at the interface of medical practice and management is hard. In addition to the enormous effort required to acquire and retain competence in two separate areas of knowledge having absolutely nothing in common, immersion in a dual identity, as indicated by Kurtz (1994), is emotionally and physically exhausting. Extending competence and credibility on one side often detracts from one's effectiveness in the other. Many of the traditional emotional and cognitive properties essential to succeed in medicine are impediments to effective managerial performance—such as consensus building, visionary strategic planning, and flexibility to deal with the unexpected. Conflicts of identity are aggravated by frequently inconsistent and contradictory organizational expectations and demands. The price of leadership, moreover, necessitates a degree of detachment from one's medical colleagues that contributes to feelings of isolation and loneliness (Kurtz 1994; Thompson 1991).

Research findings conclude that individuals drawn to medicine are too individualistic and independent to adjust well to what is required at the CEO level (Kurtz 1994; Peters 1994; O'Connor and Shewchuk 1993). Physicians tend to be crisis-oriented, whereas senior executives need to focus on the attainment of long-term goals. Clinicians are inclined to prefer immediate gratification and the satisfaction of tangible results; in contrast, general managers are enamored with processes in which the results of their labors generally are hidden and only emerge over long periods. Other ill-fitting characteristics include an authoritarian interpersonal relations style that deters delegation and the acceptance of others as equals; and a narrow concentrated intellectual focus suitable for knowing a lot about a single subject, instead of a broader mindset conducive to knowing a little about many subjects (Kurtz 1994; Peters 1994; O'Connor and Shewchuk 1993; Ottensmeyer and Key 1994; McCall and Clair 1992).

Physicians also are believed to be uncomfortable with abstract-conceptual aspects of community issues and political maneuvering. Nor are they thought to be very introspective (Kurtz 1994; Peters 1994; O'Connor and Shewchuk 1993; Ottensmeyer and Key 1994; McCall and Clair 1992). CEOs incapable of understanding their own internal and external sources of power as well as those of others are at a serious disadvantage. It helps also to be able to anticipate the demands of competing interest groups and unstable power coalitions if one is to effectively carry out the negotiations and bargaining enabling the restoration of normal working relationships in the midst of disagreement and conflict. In the world of high-level management, compromise is considered an art and a virtue, unlike in the practice of medicine where it is seen as a sign of weakness (Zuckerman and Dowling 1997).

Whatever their academic credentials, physicians aspiring to become CEOs have numerous obstacles to overcome. One of the hardest adjustments involves the difference in rationality separating medical from managerial decision making. Whereas clinicians are taught to rely on fact, linearity, and logic, managers follow a highly amorphous cognitive pathway, because the bulk of their decisions entail getting people of diverse backgrounds and interests to act on a course of action that often supersedes the presence of a technically satisfactory solution (Ottensmeyer and Key 1994). The difficulty of transcending this gap is compounded by a lack of consensus, as noted by Vinson (1994), on just what physicians need to know about management and how to acquire it as they move out of constricted medical management positions into broader areas of authority. Available academic offerings typically reflect the convictions of educators in business and health administration programs, who often are too dogmatic and ill-informed to understand what is most germane to the actual responsibilities of physician CEOs in the different stages of managed care or integrated system development.

Managed Care Era Management Challenges

Heretofore, physician and nonphysician relations were quite straightforward and tranquil. The health economy prior to managed care thrived on a symbiotic connection between physicians and hospitals. Health services management, largely dominated by nonphysicians with master's degree in health administration, maintained a low profile and a benign influence. From a physician's standpoint, management at its worst was an irritating but innocuous presence.

Until the past decade or so, hospital administration consisted mainly of facilities management and the provision of ancillary business and general support services for self-employed physicians whose clinical independence and judgment was seldom questioned. The CEO functioned mainly as a satisfier of medical staff needs, as well as a public relations spokesperson and fundraiser. Consistent with historical custom, the local hospital was viewed as a community resource placed at the disposal of physicians, who were permitted to regard it as their personal workshop in return for an implied obligation to care for the indigent sick and for the performance of other charitable functions. A well-equipped and successfully managed acute facility was fundamental to attracting high-quality physicians into the locality to meet the care needs of private-pay patients. Not-for-profit designation and governance by voluntary trustees underscored the hospital's community mission to extend the area's medical resources and to provide the opportunity for physicians to practice high-quality medicine. For the most part, however, the hospital's organizational goals and activities were secondary to the fulfillment of the medical staff's professional priorities (Starr 1982; Jonas 1977).

The relationship was mutually rewarding in financial terms, because under open-ended, fee-for-service payment, hospitals derived the bulk of their income from inpatient services. Physicians profiting from these services naturally were motivated to keep hospitals full. Because of the revenues physicians produced in admissions and treatment, noninterference in clinical matters was standard hospital policy (Starr 1982; McCall and Clair 1992). In addition to sizable income disparities, differences in status and prestige contributed to managerial deference to medical authority. Clinical freedom was buttressed by widespread public awe of the esoteric nature of medical knowledge. As long as physicians practiced within tolerable professional and community norms, their clinical judgment was unquestioned.

Severance of this symbiotic relationship, of course, accounts for much of the turmoil currently associated with managed care. Once the transformation of the hospital bed from a profit center to a cost center occurs, managed care plans and hospital management understandably are impelled to intrude into the clinical arena. In so doing, however, it is essential that they avoid incurring the enmity of the medical community because of the power physicians hold with respect to patient admissions and treatment. Nothing is more predictive of failure than a high-handed management that considers physicians the source of its problems instead of an integral part of their solution.

Illustrative of some of the more counterproductive and self-destructive actions to be avoided are the imposition of clinical guidelines without medical staff participation, monitoring and evaluating physician performance by clinically unqualified persons, expanding the scope of nonmedical clinicians and alternative medicine practitioners during times of physician anxiety over income and job security, and infliction of unpopular performance-based compensation and income redistribution schemes. Only hubris and ignorance can explain why nonphysician administrators might fail to realize their vulnerability and expendability and invite unnecessary confrontation and deadlock in dealing with highly contentious physician issues.

The reality that only physicians are allowed to practice medicine and that they can use this power to assist or subvert organizational objectives strongly suggests that physicians eventually will displace nonphysicians in top management positions and gives credence to scenarios whereby professionally trained nonphysician administrators increasingly will be demoted to secondary supportive functions. According to such thinking, physician leadership will be preferred in institutional settings where medical education, research, and advanced tertiary services are paramount in relationships among major medical centers and community hospitals, and nonphysicians will be favored as chief operating officers in integrated health networks and as CEOs in a majority of smaller community hospitals. Admittedly highly plausible, such predictions, nonetheless, require qualification, for life at the top may prove no less perilous and short-lived for physicians than for nonphysicians. Multiprofessional consensus decision-making arrangements whereby nonphysician and physician managers share power and work in adjacent offices is highly appealing in theory. In practice, however, the proclivities of individuals socialized in clinical decision making may impede constructive engagement of amorphous strategic planning and political leadership issues. Such differences in orientation lend themselves to a division of labor where nonphysicians occupy top CEO positions and physician managers assume the duties of chief operating officers in charge of the organization's day-to-day activities.

But even in this connection, possession of a medical degree conveys limitations. While advantageous in many operational areas, a clinical mindset is unconducive to dealing properly with complex personnel and human relations problems requiring strong interpersonal and communication skills. Leading rank-and-file physicians, for example, can be especially difficult for senior physician managers, who, typically, are older than their subordinates and often insensitive to intergenerational differences in acquiescence to authority, financial security needs, lifestyle values, and other contentious matters.

To succeed as a CEO, a physician must endure an inordinate amount of role conflict. Conceivably, the exigencies of clinical medicine and organizational bottom-line objectives need not be at cross-purposes, but harmony will prove illusive, except possibly in the long run when managed care enters a more advanced and stable stage. Meanwhile, acrimony and discord more often will be the rule rather than the exception as long as purchasers continue to squeeze managed care to demonstrate that it can save money in ways other than through selective enrollment and the curtailment of unnecessary hospital days. Inevitably, managed care plans are compelled to address the more difficult tasks of altering physician practice patterns and cutting clinical payroll expenditures. But this is easier said than done.

Whether armed with a management degree or not, physician executives will be hard pressed to overcome the effects of socialization that predisposes them to subordinate organizational objectives to clinical values and patient advocacy. This is but an extension of a much larger dilemma. To maintain competence and credibility in both medicine and management, they need to remain deeply immersed in both without impairing their standing and effectiveness with constituencies in each of the two vastly different arenas. Cooperation requires a degree of identification with one area that can undermine their ability to lead in the other (Ottensmeyer and Smith 1994; Leatt 1994). Even when physician executives succeed in disassociating themselves from medical loyalties and peer attachments, circumstances will arise when a board of directors instinctively believes that a nonphysician is a better choice for certain difficult undertakings, such as lowering the compensation of medical personnel, reducing the number of clinical staff, or negotiating reimbursement contracts with third party payors.

Individuals attracted to medicine are not inclined to excel at business any more than individuals drawn to business are suited by intellect and personality to succeed in medicine. Prolonged education and training in clinical subjects is a further deterrent to physicians' succeeding in business. At a time when corporate aspects of healthcare are becoming more complicated, the individuals best positioned to lead are those who not only have the proper training but also work at improving their management skills full time.

Although the business orientation of nonphysicians appears more compatible with the early stages of managed care, when the emphasis is on managing money, and the clinical orientation of physicians seems better matched to the priorities of managed care in the intermediate development stage, neither has a clear-cut advantage once managed care reaches full maturity. (A major exception to this generalization exists in teaching and research centers, where physicians may continue to have an edge in CEO selection.) When population-based health services and cost control become the overriding managed care goals, clinical knowledge is instrumental but insufficient. Total healthcare management requires not only a different skill mix, but also a broader mindset, for which, according to Kindig (1997), appropriate educational preparation and training is not readily available in the conventional medical school.

As indicated by Carol (1997), a background in hospital administration is equally insufficient. It may be more of a hindrance than an asset. Hospitals function as a top-down hierarchy where people are managed and evaluated individually and motivated by good performance reviews and annual salary increases. Little of this is relevant to an advanced managed care setting where individuals work as teams, executives manage across rather than down the organization, and incentives must encompass both payor and patient satisfaction in addition to raising the health status of enrolled populations.

Much of management education today appears antiquated, and it bears a closer relationship to the past than to contemporary realities. The advent of integrated delivery systems and the multifaceted objectives of rapidly maturing managed care initiatives signal a need for more comprehensive and coherent instruction. Along with felicity in business management, relevant clinical knowledge, and community medicine methods, effective executive leadership in the managed care era requires an acuity of mind and tolerance for ambiguity in dealing with multiple boards of trustees, organizations with different religious affiliations, and medical groups. In such highly charged political settings, team building rather than authority wielding and bureaucratic personalities are better equipped to succeed. Given the more sophisticated technical and leadership qualifications demanded, the separation of graduate management training now existing in schools of public health, medicine, and business and health administration is outdated.

Clearly, such division runs counter to effective functioning of shared management and multidisciplinary problem-solving teams that are increasingly useful, if not essential, for addressing the proliferation of complicated issues of productivity and quality improvement in frequently anomalous circumstances. Insofar as feasible, persons entering management from different disciplinary backgrounds will be better prepared for leadership if given the opportunity to sit together in the same classroom, where they can learn from one another and establish foundations for more constructive multiprofessional decision making.

Such a program of study, however, must be sufficiently flexible to serve the needs of physicians requiring deeper exposure to management and leadership studies and those of nonphysicians requiring an intelligent understanding of the natural history of disease and the relationship between clinical decision making and cost effectiveness and quality of healthcare. Shared experiences and mutual aid in learning the language and methods of managerial decision making, along with the arcane arts of leadership and good patient care practice, would do much to lessen the propensity of physician and nonphysician managers to view themselves as separate and special elites with special values that inhibit cross-disciplinary understanding and cooperation.

Concluding Comments

The issue of who will lead rapidly evolving managed care corporations is not easily resolved. It is not preordained that physician managers will dominate the CEO ranks, but they do have a competitive edge. Their qualifications undoubtedly are better matched to the central issues determining the viability of managed care organizations currently and in the foreseeable future. Also, much hinges on the preferences of employers, who in many instances will be drawn to the positive spill-overs to their organization from the status and prestige physicians generally command in public opinion and among the politically powerful. Nonphysician managers, in comparison, may be viewed as a liability, insofar as they have less credibility and influence with physicians conducting patient care and with other vital clinical personnel. Equally if not more important, nonphysician managers lack the technical know-how for cutting costs without doing harm to the quality of care.

Experience may show, however, that too much is expected of medical leadership and that, by itself, it provides employers with an incomplete formula for achieving desired organizational objectives. As a practical matter, physician executives will not be able to avoid getting caught in the crossfire of inconsistent and contradictory demands arising within and among special interest groups situated in clinical and financial spheres and in external constituencies promulgating larger community priorities. Achieving and maintaining a harmonic relationship with medical peers within the confines of managed care is complicated by the heterogeneity of concerns within the medical community, leading to frequent infighting between primary care practitioners and subspecialists and between clinically engaged and population-focused physicians (Aluise, Vaughan, and Vaughan 1994; Lyons and Cejka 1994).

However favorable the physician CEO impression among board members, prestige and status are highly ephemeral. In the final analysis, performance will count for far more than imagery. Early depletion of political capital and disappointment with physician CEO results, ironically, could contribute to increased opportunities for nonphysicians at the top of tomorrow's managed care organizations.

Who will actually lead may closely parallel experience in other sectors of the economy where, depending on the nature of prevailing problems and opportunities, the CEO title is given variously to individuals with competency in production, marketing, and finance. Despite the continuation of disciplinary and interpersonal rivalries, an atmosphere of cooperation and mutual support prevails in these settings because of the influence of organizational reward systems and the exercise of enlightened self-restraint. Thus, in managed care, organizations experiencing trouble with profitability naturally will seek someone with financial prowess who can also lead, while an organization encountering trouble with regulatory agencies will search for a CEO with political sophistication.

In the matter of healthcare, discerning governing boards understand that each discipline, as a consequence of specialization and immersion in a professional culture, is afflicted with a certain amount of trained incapacity as well as competitive strengths. Although not always, when physicians are in charge, the quality of care goes up but so do the costs; conversely, when nonphysicians are in charge, efficiency may increase but so also does a fixation on short-term results and insensitivity to the humanitarian dimensions of patient care and community medicine (Wilson and Schroeder 1992).

When all is said and done, formal training and qualification may count for less than mindset and interpersonal chemistry. Regardless of educational degree and work experience, some individuals have what it takes and others do not. In leadership selection, the prudent rule of thumb among savvy employers is to prefer those who do and to avoid those who do not.

The complex demands of healthcare delivery being what they are, a winner-take-all approach in jockeying for leadership positions is dysfunctional. The key to survival and prosperity is not control but cooperation and teamwork. Teamwork, trust, and recognition are enlightened pathways by which staff potential is fulfilled. As recognized by Maslow (1965) several decades ago, and now being rediscovered (Petzinger 1997), teams make better performers and better performers make better teams. Enlightened management is keenly alert to the payoff from delegation and the likelihood that the more influence and power it distributes to others, the more it acquires for itself. Much of the unrest associated with leadership struggles may be averted through innovative approaches to the structure of authority that are more closely attuned to the unique powers physicians have in matters pertaining to cost-effective methods for delivering care and controlling quality.

Possibly more than any other factor, the future of integrated health systems and managed care will be decided by the extent to which principles of enlightened leadership are appreciated and followed throughout the organization. In this context, neither physician managers nor nonphysician managers are destined to dominate totally the top executive positions in the rapidly changing health field. Each brings advantages and shortcomings to the management table. Advancement of their self-interests and those of the organization they serve depends on the synergy possible from a policy of mutual cooperation and trust.

Acknowledgment

The authors are indebted to Lynn Smaha, M.D., Ph.D., President, Guthrie Clinic, Sayre, Pennsylvania, for sharing the governance model formulation based on his medical group's relationship with PhyCor, one of the nation's largest physician practice management companies.

References

Aluise, J., R. Vaughan, and M. Vaughan. 1994. "The New Health Care Civilization: Integration of Physician Land and Manageria." *Physician Executive* 20 (7): 3–8.

American Medical Association, Council on Ethical and Judicial Affairs Report. 1995. "Ethical Issues in Managed Care." *Journal of the American Medical Association* 273 (4): 330–39.

Anders, G., and L. McGinley. 1997. "A New Brand of Crime Now Stirs the Feds: Health Care Fraud." *Wall Street Journal*, May 6, 1997.

Anonymous. 1997. "Data Watch: Public-Private About Face." *Business and Health* 15 (4): 82.

Battistella, R. 1997. "The Political Economy of Health Services: A Review and Assessment of Major Ideological Influences and the Impact of New Economic Realities." In *Health Politics and Policy*, 3rd ed., edited by T. Litman and L. Robins. Albany, NY: Delmar.

Battistella, R., and T. Weil. 1986. "Pro-Competitive Health Policy: Benefits and Perils." *Frontiers of Health Services Management* 2 (4): 3–27.

———. 1996. "The New Management Competencies: A Global Perspective." *Physician Executive* 22 (7): 18–23.

Brown, L. 1983. *Politics and Health Care Organization: HMOs as Federal Policy.* Washington, DC: Brookings Institution.

Carol, R. 1997. "Skills for a New Marketplace." *Healthcare Executive* 12 (1): 17–22.

Claxton, G., J. Feder, D. Schactman, and S. Altman. 1997. "Public Policy Issues in Nonprofit Conversions: An Overview." *Health Affairs* 16 (2): 9–28.

Cook, B. 1997. "Risks of Risk Sharing." *Modern Healthcare* 27 (14): 22–23.

Freidson, E. 1971. *Profession of Medicine.* New York: Dodd, Mead.

Fuchs, V. 1997. "Managed Care and Merger Mania." *Journal of the American Medical Association* 277 (11): 920–21.

Griffith, J. R. 1996. "Managing the Transition to Integrated Health Care Organizations." *Frontiers of Health Services Management* 12 (4): 4–50.

Hasan, M. 1996. "Let's End the Nonprofit Charade." *New England Journal of Medicine* 334 (18): 1055–57.

Herzlinger, R. 1997. *Market Driven Health Care.* Reading, MA: Addison-Wesley.

Iglehart, J. 1992. "The American Health Care System: Managed Care." *New England Journal of Medicine* 327 (10): 742–47.

Jenkins, M. (ed.). 1996. *The Managed Care Yearbook,* 3rd ed. Wall Township, NJ: Managed Care Information Center.

Jonas, S. 1977. *Health Care Delivery in the United States.* New York: Springer.

Kaiser, L. 1994. "Key Management Skills for the Physician Executive." In *New Leadership in Health Care Management: The Physician Executive,* 2nd ed., edited by W. Curry. Tampa, FL: American College of Physician Executives.

Kindig, D. 1997. "Do Physician Executives Make a Difference?" *Frontiers of Health Services Management* 13 (3): 38–42.

Krill, M. 1995. *Successful Partnerships for the Future.* Englewood, CO: Medical Group Management Association.

Kurtz, M. E. 1994. "The Dual Role Dilemma." In *New Leadership in Health Care*

Management: The Physician Executive, 2nd ed., edited by W. Curry. Tampa, FL: American College of Physician Executives.

Kuttner, R. 1997. *Everything For Sale*. New York: Alfred A. Knopf.

Lazarus, A. 1997. "Breaking the Glass Ceiling." *Physician Executive* 23 (3): 8–13.

Leatt, P. 1994. "Physicians in Health Care Management: Physicians as Managers, Roles and Future Challenges." *Journal of the Canadian Medical Association* 150 (2): 171–78.

LeTourneau, B., and W. Curry. 1997. "Physicians as Executives: Boon or Boondoggle?" *Frontiers of Health Services Management* 13 (3): 3–25.

Luke, R., and J. Begun. 1997. "Strategy Making in Health Care Organizations." In *Essentials of Health Care Management*, edited by S. Shortell and A. Kaluzny. Albany, NY: Delmar.

Lyons, M., and S. Cejka. 1994. "Getting a Firm Grip on the Realities for Physician Executives." *Physician Executive* 20 (6): 8–12.

Maslow, A. 1965. *Eupsychian Management: A Journal*. Homewood, IL: R.D. Irwin.

McArthur, J., and F. Moore. 1997. "The Two Cultures and the Health Care Revolution." *Journal of the American Medical Association* 277 (12): 985–99.

McCall, M., and J. Clair. 1990. "Why Physician Managers Fail—Part One." *Physician Executive* 16 (3): 6–10.

———. 1992. "In Transit from Physician to Manager—Part One." *Physician Executive* 18 (2): 3–9.

Mitka, M. 1994. "What You Need to Lead: Molding a Group of Headstrong Physicians into an Effective Team Takes Time, Training, and Impeccable Medical Credentials." *American Medical News* 37 (19): 29–32.

Moore, W. 1970. *The Professions*. New York: Russell Sage Foundation.

Morone, J. 1997. "Gridlock and Breakthrough in American Health Politics." In *Health Politics and Policy*, 3rd ed., edited by T. Litman and L. Robins. Albany, NY: Delmar.

Nudelman, P., and L. Andrews. 1996. "The Value Added of Not-for-Profit Health Plans." *New England Journal of Medicine* 334 (16): 1057–59.

O'Connor, S., and R. Shewchuk. 1993. "Enhancing Administrator-Clinician Relationships: The Role of Psychological Type." *Health Care Management Review* 18 (2): 57–65.

Ottensmeyer, D., and M. Key. 1994. "The Unique Contribution of the Physician Executive to Health Care Management." In *New Leadership in Health Care Management: The Physician Executive*, 2nd ed., edited by W. Curry. Tampa, FL: American College of Physician Executives.

Ottensmeyer, D., and H. Smith. 1994. "Physician Executives and Integrated Health Systems." In *New Leadership in Health Care Management: The Physician Executive*, 2nd ed., edited by W. Curry. Tampa, FL: American College of Physician Executives.

Pellegrino, E. 1986. "Rationing Health Care: The Ethics of Medical Gatekeeping." *Journal of Contemporary Health Law and Policy* 2 (2): 23–45.

Peters, R. 1994. *When Physicians Fail As Managers*. Tampa, FL: American College of Physician Executives.

Petzinger, T. 1997. "Radical Work by Guru of Leadership Takes 30 Years to Flower." *Wall Street Journal* (April 25).

Quinn, J., P. Anderson, and S. Finkelstein. 1996. "Managing Professional Intellect: Making the Most of the Best." *Harvard Business Review* 74 (2): 71–80.

Relman, A. 1991. "The Health Care Industry: Where Is It Taking Us?" *New England Journal of Medicine* 325 (12): 854–59.

———. 1992. "What Markets Are Doing to Medicine." *Atlantic Monthly* 269 (3): 99–106.

Rodwin, M. 1993. *Medicine, Money, and Morals: Physicians' Conflicts of Interest.* New York: Oxford University Press.

Shortell, S., and A. Kaluzny (eds.). 1997. *Essentials of Health Care Management.* Albany, NY: Delmar.

Shortell, S., R. Gillies, and D. Anderson. 1994. "The New World of Managed Care: Creating Organized Delivery Systems." *Health Affairs* 13 (5): 46–64.

Smaha, L. 1997. Personal communication.

Sparrow, M. 1996. *License to Steal: Why Fraud Plagues America's Heath Care System.* Boulder, CO: Westview Press.

Starr, P. 1982. *The Social Transformation of American Medicine.* New York: Basic Books.

Thompson, R. 1991. *Keys To Winning Physician Support.* Tampa, FL: American College of Physician Executives.

Vinson, C. 1994. "Administrative Knowledge and Skills Needed by Physician Executives." *Physician Executive* 20 (6): 3–7.

Walters, D. 1996. "California's Nonprofit HMOs Have Highest Medical Loss Ratios." *Managed Care Week* 6 (8): 3.

Weissenstein, E. 1996. "Average Physician Executive Salary Tops $180,000." *Modern Healthcare* 26 (6): 46.

Williams, S., and P. Torrens. 1993. "Managed Care: Restructuring the System." In *Introduction to Health Services*, 4th ed., edited by S. Williams, and P. Torrens. Albany, NY: Delmar.

Wilson, A, and N. Schroeder. 1992. "Physician and Nonphysician Managers as Decision Makers: Are the Differences Justified or Just an Illusion?" *Physician Executive* 18 (5): 3–6.

Zuckerman, H., and W. Dowling. 1997. "The Managerial Role." In *Essentials of Health Care Management*, edited by S. Shortell and A. Kaluzny. Albany, NY: Delmar.

Physician Opportunities in Management: Likely Futures

Montague Brown

HERE ARE many trends today that spell great opportunity for physicians who seek to shift their careers into management.[1] This chapter speculates on three model scenarios as the most likely directions of the healthcare system, along with their implications for physician and nonphysician executives.

Like much in life, all predictions of the future contain uncertainties and unanticipated consequences. Given the pluralistic character of our society and the fragmented form of government we have, no policy direction is every likely to be a clear representation of its supporters' principal aim.

Muddling through is our process; hybridization is our outcome. Add to this the fact that no opportunity comes without some possible negative side effects and blind alleys for the unaware. Indeed, it is the fact of negative side effects and unanticipated consequences that often justifies a healthy investment in competent management. Management generally proposes policy, boards decide, and then management tries to implement the policy and ideas in a very uncertain world.

Theoretical Considerations

There has been a great debate[2] in physics as to how the universe works. In a Newtonian universe things are orderly and regular; thus, the task for science is to determine the order and then apply it to craft logical interventions. The other major perspective—the one currently winning—is the quantum view, which says that things are basically unknowable and that, if you attempt to measure an aspect of the universe, the fact of measurement itself changes the fundamental nature of the thing being observed. This new world view is increasingly being applied to theories as to how organizations[3] and markets work. These readings are sobering to consider and freeing at the same time. It is sobering to see a clear argument and much evidence that suggest that the best-laid plans of mice and men are likely to be trashed by uncertainty. It is freeing because it opens the very real possibility that people can actually change the course of their history. It also opens the possibility that winning strategies can be developed that prevail against even more effective strategies because they gain acceptance and dominate markets early. Unfortunately, this also means that we can evolve second-rate strategies that prevail over better ones.

Put in more direct terms, a Newtonian perspective presumes that the organization of health services and the roles people play in the system are logical outcomes of some long-range plan that has been faultlessly organized. Or at least it is so to the extent that the workings of the system are correctly understood. In a management sense, this approach assumes that a master plan can be laid out on the basis of knowledge of how things work. This master plan can be implemented and followed for years with only such change as may come from new inventions.

A quantum perspective is much more problematic. The universe and how it will behave in the immediate, foreseeable, and far-flung future is essentially unknowable. However, what *is* known is that systems will tend to self-organize and that this organization can be very stable, although it is possible that even very small changes in the environment can have very large consequences. One story has it that a butterfly flapping its wings in the Andes can start a chain of interactions in the atmosphere that culminates weeks later in a tornado in Kansas. From this perspective, a prudent manager would maximize knowledge of options and possible directions. In management parlance, this approach might be labeled strategic thinking. In other words, the prudent manager would engage the broadest array of thinking available from a diverse[4] team. This team would literally engage in strategic scenario building and action as it rides the tide of daily market changes and seeks to position the organization to win against challenges to it. This would include consideration of how to win or survive under any of the scenarios discussed below.

Scenarios

Three separate scenarios are presented here to illustrate and aid in thinking about the future of physicians as executives, the traditional healthcare executive, and others who may come into the arena of top management because of their roles in bringing change. These scenarios describe forces or megatrends that can and do overlap, sometimes to good effect, at other times to the mutual disadvantage of each.

Market- and Consumer-Driven System

The first scenario is a healthcare world that is driven increasingly by a consumer-focused business-oriented revolution.[5] As entrepreneurs sense the potential for making profits in healthcare from redesigning the delivery of health services around market concepts of convenience, value (a function of usefulness and cost) drives services. The argument for such a system is based heavily on the notion that markets serving customers will ultimately function to drive business toward vendors who provide the kinds of values that customers seek. A small debate on an Internet discussion group highlights a small move in this direction: Apparently, there is a hospital that advertises that people will be seen within 30 minutes in its emergency department. It seems that, in this market, waiting times in the busier places could run to several hours. One ethicist was quoted as saying that such an introduction would overturn time-tested professional principles of seeing those most in need first. An emergency department physician apparently thought that it violated professional principles as well, while the business organization that instituted the procedure saw it as a straightforward response to a market opportunity. Apparently, the 30-minute guarantee caused a downturn in people going to hospitals that made no such offer and an increase in visits to the one that did. Patients apparently prefer convenience—*their* convenience—not that of professionals or other patients.

In a market-oriented system, one pays close attention to what customers want and tries to provide it. One physician[6] colleague actually provides visits free to his patients if he runs more than ten minutes late. Although the physician's practice has few emergencies, this physician is practicing market-oriented medicine. There is no particular magic to thinking through what might fit into this category or approach; all one needs to do is to go through one or more encounters with the current system of care to find many things needing attention.

One executive, who opened some of the early convenience-oriented "doc in a box" clinics, indicated that his research suggested that the average walk-in customer would or could spend as much in one encounter as the average Tiffany customer.[7] For this, he said, much could be done better, more conveniently, and at a good profit. I believe that his effort failed to succeed, but the idea continues to be accepted in many markets.

The vision care business is also an example of this approach. The customer can walk in; get an eye examination, usually with little wait; and then have the prescription filled within two hours. Convenience wins handily against price, which is lower if one is willing to go to several places and wait some days for the finished product. The last time I stopped at my local vision shop, the optometrist had a new camera to take a picture of the back of the eye. I bought the picture to have such a record against which to judge later changes. After finding that my vision had changed too little to require new glasses, I got the slightly revised prescription and then went over to the other side of the store to get my current glasses tightened up a bit and cleaned . . . at no charge.

In Tucson, Arizona, as in a number of other cities, a new Heart Specialty Hospital is under construction. For routine cases, it will try to cluster services, cater to the various physicians involved, and seek to provide very friendly, focused services to customers who need this service. While this is a powerful idea, not many have approached it from a traditional acute care hospital base. It is business-oriented individuals who seek to exploit markets for services. They see potential for profit from organization and delivery of health services that most professional healthcare executives would find hard to imagine and nearly impossible to accomplish, given the fact that most currently are employed in the very organizations that benefit most from not changing.

Managed care is a market-oriented phenomenon. While nearly all traditional health insurance firms today have adopted managed care as their primary mode of operation, it was the entrepreneurial firms that broke down barriers to its introduction. Some of these entrepreneurs came from traditional health administration and health insurance ranks. Many of the early models were not-for-profit and federally financed. As they succeeded and needed capital to expand, the executives pushed to take the HMOs private and secure venture capital to expand. What began as an innovative idea, intended to inject a new form of competition into the health service system, quickly became a captive of the marketplace. In this case, the market was primarily employers who desperately wanted to reduce the cost of care. Managed care does this, but whether the current gains can be sustained without fundamentally reengineering the delivery system remains to be seen. Any organization that makes its money by not providing care and then asks consumers to choose a panel of physicians before those consumers know their medical needs leaves much to be desired.

Because managing the way in which physicians deliver care is at the heart of what HMOs need to be doing, physicians find many roles in this part of the industry. Again, however, physicians find their primary role on the provider relations side of the equation, not on the risk assessment, finance, or marketing sides. Even here, physicians will tend to be slotted into roles associated with their particular medical expertise. I see this as current reality—and neither good nor bad per se. If a physician gains expertise in other areas, there may still be a tendency for others to perceive him or her as a physician first and as a finance officer/lawyer/executive second. What the long-term perception will be will probably depend heavily on which skills and knowledge base are used.

Challenging the status quo is a sport more easily practiced from a position of studied ignorance of why existing arrangements are sacred. This provides the entrepreneur an advantage when pattern-breaking change is required. Of course, some physicians are themselves pattern breakers and entrepreneurs, and they can and will lead some of these efforts. But for the physician making an incremental shift from clinical work to overseeing or dealing with issues central to clinical work, no major leadership role will likely be forthcoming. Of course, small steps in the leadership hierarchy may eventually lead to major leadership positions, and people doing outstanding work in relatively minor positions are sometimes promoted to major leadership positions. Never say never.

Entrepreneurial health professionals can and do make some of these kinds of moves. As insiders, physicians have special insights into patient needs and have an edge in patient confidence in what they do. However, the insider often comes with a lot of assumptions about what can and cannot be done, which can severely limit what they will think possible. The outsider entrepreneur comes without many of the preconceived notions about what can be done and thus may have an edge in seeing new possibilities. Teaming the two kinds of advantages presents a more likely winning combination. Once an innovation has been shown to work, insiders may have an advantage in moving it forward quickly. So who will lead in this model? Physicians and outsiders who each know how and when to use each other's expertise and insights.

Competing Organized Delivery Systems

A second, and currently the most popular, approach to making healthcare more affordable is to professionally design, organize, and deliver vertically integrated care systems linked through collaboration, ownership, and coordination[8] and to implement regional integrated delivery systems. In these systems, professional managers in partnership with medical staffs and physicians participating in the management and governance of the evolving systems have key roles. Hospitals merge and physicians consider group practices, tight networks, employment within systems, and generally a collaborative role, albeit close to the more traditional role of physicians.

This scenario has the major advantage of being the strategy of choice for most if not all of the major hospitals and for many of the medical school teaching facilities in the nation. This option expands role, influence, range of services, and ability to gain managed care contracts for the surviving systems.[9] As organized systems gain power in the marketplace, many have invested in managed care functions, including insurance risk products and direct contracting with employers, thus bypassing insurers and managed care plans. This model has been pioneered by prepaid group practices such as Kaiser Permanente and a consumer cooperative, Group Health Cooperative of Puget Sound. These organizations built on growth only for integrated services. For those services either too complex or rarely utilized, these organizations typically contract out for what they cannot provide. Services are typically added only after the enrolled population base is of sufficient size to support them. Others in the industry that try to copy this model, especially large hospitals, have a very difficult time because they must attract patients from a far larger population base than they can capture quickly in a capitated model of care. This direction of integration is consistent with the current movement and, to the extent that it succeeds, will become the norm.

Several factors make it difficult to integrate fully all of the services in a major market. First, there are legal prohibitions that make it difficult to achieve market dominance through mergers and acquisition. More important, many buyers are suspicious of any organization that might possess monopoly power that eliminates price competition among competitors. Second, entrepreneurs who see many ways in which they can carve out lucrative pieces of the healthcare business often supply the service more efficiently and in ways more attractive to consumers.

The organized delivery system approach has much in common with the third scenario—a national healthcare system dominated principally by government. Private not-for-profit or for-profit systems that achieve market dominance have some of the attributes of a government-dominated system. When consumers have few or no choices, it is possible to reduce duplication and achieve economies of resource use. Theoretically, this will lower costs to consumers, thus achieving the oft-stated goal of high-value, low-cost, high-quality services.[10] To achieve many of these economies in a world with excess capacity, the more integrated systems must either convince some of their constituents to downsize or they must compete so effectively against other systems that they force their competitors to downsize. As one might easily imagine, it is a lot easier to merge than it is to get a decision to unilaterally close. And it is often easier to subsidize inefficiencies than it is to get elements of a system to reduce voluntarily the work they do and the services they provide.

The organized system approach has worked well to contain costs in countries such as the United Kingdom (U.K.), where the government establishes the areas and populations to be served by a system of health services and then proceeds to ration carefully the amount and types of services that can be offered. To make this kind of rationing work, it is essential that physicians are partners in getting patients to comply with the restrictions involved. With such a collaboration essential, it should come as no surprise that, in the U.K., the chief medical officer and the chief administrative officer have equal access to boards and to policymaking within a system.

In the United States, organized delivery systems lack the requisite mandate or franchise to serve a specified population and thus are in no position to ration or limit resources to get maximum efficiency from their use. Thus, one major element associated with the low cost of organized delivery systems in the U.K. is missing in the United States.[11] Managed care firms compete, and contracts are often for one year at a time, making the contract term too short to fully count on the volumes, revenues, and potential profits from any investment that needs more than a year to pay off.

Physician executives in these fledgling U.S. organized delivery systems gain easy access into managerial ranks by way of quality control, negotiating relations in preferred provider organizations, and the myriad other details required to coordinate large, complex systems. In at least the early systems that were developed around physician group practices, physicians have prominent roles in management and governance. This does not, however, take them directly to the executive suite. For the most part, executives trained in traditional health administration, often in business schools, will generally keep physician executives in more specialized roles dealing primarily with other physicians, thus maintaining the larger, more generalist roles for themselves. This type of limiting behavior is not restricted to physicians. Nurses, finance officers, and others find themselves pigeonholed, as well.[12] This should be no surprise to anyone working in the health field, especially physicians, who dominate some of the most important elements and reserve decisions to themselves against all challengers. On the other hand, as physicians enter executive roles and gain business school and health administration training, more will eventually compete for chief executive roles within organized delivery systems. With some younger physicians, gaining an M.B.A. or some other management degree will place them early on dual tracks that could lead to greater leadership roles.

Government-Dominated System

A third option is one that moves increasingly toward a government-dominated system. Health policy in the United States seems to move in disjointed and incremental ways. The Clinton administration proposed a comprehensive national system of health services to be overseen by regional boards with authority to direct overall policy in coordination with other government policies—in short, a national health plan. While this approach was defeated as an overall package, recent events suggest that those who favor a national health system are now moving to get it via incremental reforms.[13] Such a system would likely move first to a national health insurance system, with many of the smaller insurers dropping out and only large companies surviving. Regional planning and delivery system oversight by government-appointed boards will consist of persons representing the public, professions, and unions.

Government systems will seek an organizational level for regional boards, and an attempt will be made to ration technology and services to fit the needs of the defined regional population. All government payors will limit their payments to services and vendors approved by the regional system. Because the system starts out as a pluralistic system with many types of ownership, control will be through careful restrictions on approvals of services and through payment only to approved vendors. Because the United States has adopted many techniques for rationing services via managed care, those techniques will continue to be applied. A long-term ratcheting down of the system will make it somewhat more efficient and will stifle any further innovation associated with the market-driven model, except for services not covered by the national system.

Government systems will be politically well balanced, so the medical profession will likely have a major role in such systems, but they are at the same time likely to be teamed with those professionally trained in management, nursing, and professions representing other elements of the voting strength within the health service establishment. Physicians will find employment opportunities as executives in many areas of such systems. And, given their potential political influence many, with carefully built-up management credentials, should achieve the highest ranks of management.

Prospects for Each Scenario
Market and Consumer Scenario

Every major aspect of healthcare today is experiencing growth in the role of market-oriented firms and of Wall Street capital. Managed care has moved from a major entrepreneurial movement to a point where very large, established insurance companies and the Blue Cross plans have absorbed these new methods and the companies that established them to make managed care the principal mode of supplying health insurance.

Governments are privatizing more health and welfare functions, with Medicaid being rapidly converted to a market-oriented, managed care environment.[14] This movement follows trends in the private sector and has been fueled by the welfare reform movement, which emphasizes more state control of such services, although most of the privatization of Medicaid has been done using waivers from federal requirements.

Medical care delivery is being radically changed by Wall Street capital and by entrepreneurial firms playing a major role in every sector. Major change is occurring in the ownership and control of physician practices, community and university hospitals, and managed care companies.[15] These changes are offering physicians an opportunity to own equity shares in community hospitals, in managed care companies, in networks, and in their own practices, once they sell out to other entities. These are not merely locally owned business opportunities; these frequently are market equity firms whose stock is traded daily on national exchanges.

As these ventures emerge, physicians in coordinating, managing, and leadership roles get substantial opportunity to gain management roles as well as ownership roles. When physicians own such organizations,[16] they have great opportunities to gain stature as managers. Indeed, some will not only grow in managerial and executive stature, but they will also own substantial shares in the new firms, making it possible and desirable for them to retain major executive and governance roles when their firms go public or are sold to public firms.

Some of the major growth in the investor-owned sector is not major change in the overall distribution of services between the not-for profit public and investor-owned sector; it is more an artifact of how public equity markets behave. Many healthcare firms achieve their rapid growth by merging and acquiring existing operations. The stock market amply rewards strong, robust growth, but markets also fluctuate and trends change. Some of the robust growth companies in the 1970s and early 1980s found their stock values languishing, so company executives, in conjunction with venture capitalists, bought the company stock and took the companies private using equity capital and large amounts of debt. To pay off the debt, many elements of the firms were sold off, with each of the sold elements becoming a new, growth-oriented company. As stock prices recovered in the late 1980s, many of these firms have been recombined into even larger firms.[17] No doubt this cycle will recur periodically.

Vertical Integration and Organized Delivery Systems

No subject is hotter today than the concept of vertical integration. For many, this term means merging or melding of physician practices and hospital organizations. Sometimes physicians acquire hospitals; sometimes roles are reversed. There is also an element of integration, with physicians building and operating managed care firms. And integration occurs when insurers and managed care firms acquire and operate physician practices within their managed care operations.

Physicians serve as CEOs of many of the regional vertically integrated firms when physicians are fully integrated into the system. Many play medical director roles and roles in quality assurance. In more entrepreneurial firms, physicians are active in acquisition of practices in new markets. The greater the mixing of physicians within the integrated organization, the more likely it is that they will play leading roles.

This major strategic direction is the principal approach of most—if not all—of the voluntary sector of healthcare today. The approach has a major appeal for community-based organizations. While it requires merging many interests, it holds the promise of local control. Many of those pursuing the strategy have made substantial compromises on future action to secure partners, making one main strength (one large provider system) and at the same time a weakness (a large system with many commitments not to change dramatically.)

While large and potentially cumbersome regional integrated firms have drawbacks, they also have substantial power to resist changes that might be sought by buyers. If such systems have cleared antitrust thresholds in their formation, they may well be major players for a long time. They may be able not only to get major managed care contracts but also to keep niche firms from stealing marketshare for limited services. For instance, a heart hospital may well be able to offer a more efficient, customer-friendly service with higher quality than can more dispersed, lower-volume programs in a variety of hospitals, but, if managed care firms are faced with large, comprehensive delivery systems that want to keep their services bundled, the specialized facility may lose some business. As this is written, much speculation exists about whether this type of pressure will be resisted successfully by buyers who might well want to avoid giving too much power to a regional conglomerate. Antitrust law may also be invoked eventually against such behaviors as being anticompetitive.

At the same time that many in the field are pursuing a strategy of pulling all services together into a more cohesive, integrated package, there are many firms working to carve out niches. The marketplace is rich with opportunities in either direction.

Government-Dominated System

At this point, it appears that the federal government will move toward extending benefits incrementally to ever-larger population bases. The most recent changes in public policy make it possible for persons to keep their insurance when leaving or changing jobs, albeit that there are no restrictions on how much this might cost. The next push to extend benefits seems to be through a tobacco tax to help pay for children not eligible for Medicaid but without insurance. As this is being written, a major campaign seems to be developing to make the public aware that brain development is critical during the first three or so years of life and that the government needs to address this issue. (I interpret this as extending programs to cover life from zero to three or four years). The compromise seems to want to nationalize incrementally and then offer delivery through private and state programs with minimum federal interference—financing and, point of continuing debate, standards.

Another point coming into focus on the nationalization front is the growing concern by consumers (and their professional legal and medical advocates) that managed care might not offer sufficient options and service. So it looks as if there is going to be a federalization of the benefits package—no drive-through mastectomies or two-day hospital stays for deliveries. As with most health legislation, a problem emerges, gets national attention, and then gets political support.

Thus, at this juncture, several strands seem evident, including a federal role in benefits, federal financing for select groups, more mandates for private expenditures, and more of a role for states in managing expenditures and delivery. Physicians with public health administration degrees will play important roles in the oversight agencies that regulate healthcare services. But just as physicians face stiff competition for CEO slots from traditional health administrators and business executives in the nonpublic sector, so too will they face competition in the public sector from others trained in the public health disciplines associated with regulation and policy.

Overall Assessment

Market- and consumer-oriented firms will increasingly dominate the landscape through niche organizations and through acquisition of not-for-profit and public systems unable to achieve operating efficiencies because of political and organizational problems associated with having too many constituents to satisfy on every decision. These new firms will face competition from copycats who will emerge as soon as a new niche becomes evident. Mergers, buyouts, privatization, and other financial maneuvers will keep this new sector volatile. As the more traditional, market-oriented drug and supplier firms see pressures on their sales and prices, they too will invest in ventures that put them closer to the end user. While this activity is not widespread as yet, one cancer drug firm has a major stake in a cancer service and is expected to move to control the actual delivery of the service using its own products. While this may or not work, the interesting fact from the standpoint of this analysis is that it is being tried. More innovation can be expected. Some of it will survive.

Community organizations will continue to build ever more comprehensive organizations to try to dominate their markets to protect the ability of the system to better determine its future. Unfortunately, such systems face a huge capital hurdle. To build systems, megadoses of new capital are required for managed care, physician acquisition, and information systems. Even those that succeed in the short run face the task of maintaining sufficient growth to satisfy market pressures from adjacent markets, local competitors, and new firms trying to operate in profitable niches.

Increasingly, it appears we have reached a watershed in health policy. New national financing will be developed for special groups, with extensions of coverage and requirements for care standards liberally laced with employer mandates. There will be more national standards, with increased responsibility for state regulation and oversight. The private sector will get a larger role in provision of care, with managed care firms playing the monitoring role played in other countries by the state.

Overall, the next decade will be dominated by increased privatization of health services with capital financing from Wall Street, with all of the implications of moving toward a more business-, market-, and consumer-oriented system of health services.

It remains unclear just how much of a role will be played by the consumers, those actually needing and getting services. They will get care, but they will be greatly constrained in how, when, and where such care is actually delivered. This diminution of the role of patients as consumers bodes ill for the system and may well contain the seeds of the ultimate surrender of the entire system of health service to some national authority.

In our current system, managed care is driven by employer desires to hold down costs. Our tax codes treat employer payments for health insurance as a taxable deduction, while individuals must first pay taxes on income and cannot deduct their health insurance premiums. Thus, we are locked into a system of employer-dominated choice of health plans. Even when employers offer a choice of managed care plans, it is impossible for the typical consumer to pick a plan that will have the best qualified professionals to care for his or her needs. Why is this selection difficult? Because most people simply cannot predict what medical condition will arise during the course of time for which they have contracted with a single plan. In other words, a rational choice of plans is difficult because of the nature of the plans themselves. Individual consumers get very little choice as to what they can and cannot do.

Medicare, on the other hand, allows consumers full choice of providers and the option of going directly to specialists. As people find themselves denied proper care, they will demand and get more and more government regulation to avoid some of the harshest elements of the current systems. And as this happens, people will begin to realize that Medicare, a government program, allows precisely the kind of choice that rational consumers will want. Of course, Congress recently pushed for changes in Medicare that will encourage more seniors to go into managed care plans, thus denying this ultimate choice of providers at the point when more certain knowledge of one's condition is present. It is possible to debate the ultimate outcome, but as long as the public is aware of major barriers to choice when it really counts, political pressures will exist to increase government regulation. Whether one thinks we have nationalized healthcare may be a moot point, as government mandates grow. Privatization is occurring simultaneously with efforts by government to specify more and more of the means and ends of our health system.

A Theoretical Perspective

Every move by one player in the system affects others. In health services, we can see, at least dimly, how the myriad forces in our political system came together to blunt a drive for major healthcare reform. Prior to the Clinton administration, it was widely believed that, without presidential leadership, health reform would not happen but, with it, it was not only possible but inevitable. While the jury may still be out on the administration's impact, it could be argued that no president did more to make sure that healthcare would evolve more as a market-oriented system. While we now can say with near certainty that the system will be market- and business-oriented, it could well take a very different turn. The current system stresses provision of minimum care and limited choice of providers. While this happens all the time in government systems such as that in the U.K., in this country it flies in the face of two intractable foes: individual consumers who ultimately want choice when faced with major problems, and providers, especially physicians, who want to play a dominant role in that choice. Together with the right mix of anecdotal evidence of system shortcomings, we can and, I think, likely will have another turn in health affairs toward a national system.

What we end up with ultimately may well look like regional monopolies governed by public utility commissions, with everyone within the region guaranteed access to essentially the same kinds of services at similar prices with some limited ability to jump to other regions for more specialized services. Given the ability of small events to have major effects over time, more speculation on the future is probably unwarranted.

Two final points: In a universe in which the vast possibilities of interactions make prediction haphazard at best, one must always look at possibilities, make shorter-term predictions, and take action to maximize some of the higher probability outcomes. At the same time, one must be prepared to go another way if predictions are wrong. Flexibility and vigilance are winning attributes in an uncertain world.

In all of these scenarios there are major roles for physician managers and executives. Nothing in any of these scenarios suggests that, in the competition for executive positions, more traditionally trained health administrators and business and finance majors will willingly abdicate their positions or opportunities for power and economic reward to accommodate physicians. At the same time, physician competencies will be needed at critical junctures in all of these transformations. Once physicians are on managerial and executive tracks, many will have promise and will find opportunities to move ahead in a more generalized management career. This has happened with engineers, teachers, and lawyers, as well as physicians.

Opportunities

Changes in payment methodologies have made it increasingly important for hospitals to work more closely with medical staffs. With DRGs, hospitals need the understanding, support, and active involvement of medical staffs in bringing utilization patterns in line with reimbursement. The economic incentives for physicians have been insufficient to make this happen. Whenever hospitals need to reach out to physicians, they tend to go through the elected leadership, but they must increasingly utilize full-time medical directors to keep closer ties on a regular and full-time basis.

Medical directors and full-time chiefs have long been noted for helping to bring a degree of order and focus on high-quality outcomes and process in hospitals. But it has been the revolution in payment mechanisms that has brought the greatest pressure to have full-time physicians working closely with the medical staff. Anyone working in such roles has ample opportunities to observe, learn about, and emulate executive behaviors. Equally important, they have positions that can be used to justify participation, at institutional expense, in management development activities. This is a traditional route to larger preparation, which is itself a route to better jobs in the management arena.

With managed care, it has become even more important to have detailed understanding of cost and processes that drive costs. Managed care brings new role opportunities for physicians. Marketing and professional relations create other opportunities. With staff-model plans, becoming the CEO is a good prospect for the physician who has the political, policy, and executive skills necessary for the role.

Managed care also brings new opportunities for physicians associated with hospitals. Keeping track of costs, care maps, and protocols and finding ways to improve economic and quality performance in caring for patients is high on many agendas. Physicians have an edge for jobs in this arena, including CEO slots with more heavily integrated organizations with large physician components.

Beyond a career in managed care, many opportunities exist for physicians with managed care expertise who want to move back into hospitals, group practices, and other more integrated organizations. Just as lawyers often take apprentice roles as prosecutors, tax enforcers, and the like, only to return to protect the fox in the hen house, so too can physicians learn and develop in the art, craft, and management of managed care and then return to more interesting and higher-level roles in organizations that they have learned about from the outside. No doubt, there will be additional roles as regulators and government employees as the role of government expands its oversight of privatization of healthcare.

As more employers and managed care buyers seek hard evidence of quality and cost effectiveness, increasing attention will be given to quality process management tools and techniques. Physicians with an interest and training in measurement techniques, process interaction, and engineering types of skills will have ample opportunity to play leadership roles on teams and in departments pursuing this line of work.

Outside of organizations directly involved in providing care and measuring results, there are many entrepreneurial opportunities for physicians who want to supply services but not work for established organizations. Develop a new measurement tool. Develop a company that does surveys and then sells data analysis to those who need it. There are thousands of opportunities here. Some are managerial, some entrepreneurial, some policy, and many a mix of all three. In a profession increasingly policed by many outsiders, policing jobs abound.

Group practices will continue to develop and grow in size and complexity. This will mean greater opportunities for managers. Physicians have a natural opportunity to play leadership roles in such organizations but for those who aspire to long-term leadership and management roles, the watchword should be a continued quest for in-depth management training and experience, especially in areas of finance and health policy.

Helping to build networks and joint venture operations can open up many future opportunities for management roles. With an increasing trend toward vertical integration, some of these networks will become very large and complex operations. In fact, it is highly likely that some of these organizations will become giants that swallow hospitals, managed care organizations, physicians' practices, and insurance companies.

Summary

The future is ultimately unknowable, leaving us at the mercy of unforeseen events that can change everything. Fortunately, many years pass before some of the events that trigger major changes are evident. Most people can live fairly productive lives without being hurt because of missed trends.

But those who seek executive leadership positions must try to foresee change and take steps to position the organization so that, whatever change takes hold, it is possible to find ways to survive and thrive. Scenarios are useful devices for this kind of strategic thinking.

Here, three major scenarios dealing with market-oriented healthcare, professionally designed and managed organized delivery systems, and some form of national healthcare systems have been considered. The outlook in the near term is for increased growth in market-oriented health services. Community organizations will focus on building larger, more complex, and comprehensive systems, with entrepreneurs trying both this strategy and niche strategies. In fact, some will try both strategies simultaneously, perhaps in different markets. Almost everyone will try both strategies at different points in the growth in the marketplace, depending in part on what happens in the healthcare market and in part on what happens to their stock in the capital markets.

Change in every scenario provides opportunities for physicians to enter management and executive ranks. To the extent that more free market, consumer-oriented solutions prevail, opportunities will be wider and more open for those who want to compete for job opportunities. To the extent that professionally designed organized delivery systems dominate, there will be a lot more pressure to keep physicians in tracks more akin to their practice roles. (Of course this latter circumstance is one most forcefully advocated by physicians themselves in protecting their primary roles as professionals. That others copy the method is to be expected.)

Overall, it can be expected that more traditional managers and executives will welcome physicians in limited management roles but compete with them for larger, more generalized roles. With the large number of opportunities for physicians to enter management roles and the growing and readily available management education available to physicians, it seems inevitable that physicians will play increasingly important roles in healthcare, including chief executive officer.

On balance, today is an exciting time for healthcare executives. Every organization is undergoing major change.[18] Some forms are dying out, others emerging. Even those succeeding today may not survive in the next few years. There is real challenge in an industry on the threshold of such change. In some respects, the changes we face now mirror the changes in the air transport industry and in other regulated industries that have been deregulated. In other respects, healthcare is different. Medicine is the preeminent profession, independent and respected. And it is going toward an employment situation with little opportunity for solo private practice, even in independent small groups.

At the same time, genetics and created life forms are on the threshold of transforming how interventions are done. We are not merely seeing a movement to outpatient care, we are seeing the potential for truly new forms of care and intervention. At the other extreme, we see the possibility of an aging society in the next century overwhelming the healthcare system.

Physicians who wish to lead this revolution must master management and organizational design and development. Others can also do this, but none with same depth of insight into the underlying science and practice at the heart of the healthcare enterprise. On the science and medical practice front physicians will supply major leadership. On the organization and delivery front, managers, many of them physicians, will play major roles.

Notes

1. Several recent papers outline the major shifts and their likely impact on physicians. Brown, M. 1996. "The Commercialization of America's Voluntary Healthcare System." *Health Care Management Review* 21 (3): 13–18; Brown, M. 1996. "Health Care 2015: Flight of the Butterfly." *Physician Executive* 22 (1): 5–11; Brown, M. 1995. "Managed Care: Power and New Economic Relationships." *Physician Executive* 21 (12): 5–10; Brown, M. 1994. "Physician Opportunities in Management: Signs and Portents." *Physician Executive* 20 (12): 3–8.

2. There are many excellent books and papers on this debate. My favorites include Gleick, J. 1987. *Chaos*. London, England: Penguin Books; and Waldrop, M. 1992. *Complexity*. New York: Simon and Schuster.

3. See McDaniel, R. 1997. "Strategic Leadership: A View from Quantum and Chaos Theories." *Health Care Management Review* 22 (1): 21–37; and Arthur, W. 1997. *Increasing Returns and Path Dependency in the Economy*. Ann Arbor, MI: University of Michigan Press. McDaniel points out the many ways in which management theories have an embedded Newtonian world view. Arthur lays out a theoretical basis for looking at markets based on a quantum perspective.

4. *Diverse* here is meant in its fullest possible meaning. People with different competencies, different cultural perspectives, and different world views and approaches to problem solving. Not just politically correct diversity, but the widest possible range of thinking and perspectives that might contribute to considering more complex and more diverse strategies.

5. One articulate spokesperson for the likelihood of and reasons for this is Professor Regina Herzlinger of the Harvard Business School, who lays out a persuasive case for such a future in *Market-Driven Health Care*. 1997. New York: Addison-Wesley.

6. Personal discussion with physician involved. More recently, this physician has joined a Wall Street–financed firm that will bring such market-oriented approaches to women's health.

7. Personal communication in the early 1980s.

8. Professor Stephen Shortell of Northwestern University has carried out an extensive research program directed at building organized delivery systems. The organizations that are the focus of his research have long attempted to build such systems. One of his recent books, published in 1996 with Robin Gillies, David Anderson, Karen Erickson, and John Mitchell, is *Remaking Health Care in America: Building Organized Delivery Systems*. San Francisco: Jossey-Bass Publishers. John Griffith, a University of Michigan professor, has also written extensively about how to manage the community hospital more effectively. In recent years his attention has extended to a more coordinated and regionally designed and operated system of health services. Neither author carves out a role or anticipates the need for or usefulness of entrepreneurial, for-profit ventures of the type anticipated under Scenario One, where market orientation and entrepreneurs are key ingredients.

9. Naturally, when mergers and consolidation occur, not everyone remains on top of the organizational pyramid. However, in most mergers between voluntary, not-for-profit institutions, most of the work and many of the jobs are saved.

10. I use the term *theoretical* here to alert the reader deliberately that monopolies, whether government or private, do not always use their power to benefit consumers, and they may well not achieve the touted benefits they seek. Those who subscribe

to the market- or consumer-oriented theory of how things work believe that only with competition will consumer-oriented benefits be achieved. I find myself drawn increasingly to this view.

11. I have personally followed this movement attempting to develop organized, integrated delivery systems in the United States and have consistently found it lacking the internal discipline or the external constraints that might make it possible to reduce duplication sufficiently to substantially lower costs while maintaining high-quality service.

12. I have discussed this with hospital executives over the years. Most recently, I inquired as to whether one executive's finance officer would be considered for a new hospital being opened in the area. "No," he said, "that is for a generalist like me." Finance is finance. Medicine is medicine. Nursing is nursing. And, by implication, people in those occupations are by definition narrowly focused and less capable of carrying out more generalized executive tasks. Incidentally this attitude is not restricted to the not-for-profit, more traditional sector of healthcare and can be found in the for-profit sector as well.

13. Anyone interested in how this system might have been initially configured can read the many critiques of the Clinton health reform effort. For those who want to see the unfolding of healthcare reform incrementally, read about the various reforms advocated by Senator Ted Kennedy.

14. For a more comprehensive view of the privatization of public health functions see Halverson, P., and others. *Public Health and Managed Care: Implications for Privatization.* Gaithersburg, MD: Aspen Systems Corporation, in press.

15. This shift is very complex and requires more attention than can be given at this point. For a major debate on the subjects involved, see *Health Care Management Review*, Spring, Summer, and Fall 1994 issues, where Richard Johnson and Montague Brown, along with others, debate and discuss these changes.

16. A postulate of the debate I have had with Richard Johnson and others is that physicians can own and operate some of these for-profit businesses during a critical transition period from the entrepreneurial start-up phase until the firm is of sufficient size, scope, and profitability that it needs heavy capital infusion to grow and/or when the physician owners want to convert their ownership interest into stock that has a ready market to allow them to cash out at will.

17. I know of no comprehensive resource to describe all of this, but, for anyone interested in a case example, look at the history of Hospital Corporation of America, now a part of Columbia/HCA with one of the founding partners in the initial corporation serving as chairman and holding a large block of shares in the most recent iteration of this firm.

18. See Note 1 for several articles dealing with the issue of how to read these trends and what can be done to succeed in management. Get an education, go the extra mile in volunteering to take charge of change projects, and, when you see people who are really good at this game, get them to mentor you in your own development. Management is for the most part a team sport, so if you have been a solo operator in your practice, learn the rules of collaborative games. It can be fun, productive, and ultimately good for the people you seek to serve.

About the Editors

Barbara LeTourneau, M.D., M.B.A., CPE, FACPE, is Vice President, Medical Affairs, Northern Region, Allina Health System, Fridley, Minnesota. Over the past ten years she has had a variety of management roles with the integrated healthcare system and its predecessor organizations. She is currently President of the American College of Physician Executives (ACPE) and has served on its board of directors for the past five years. Dr. LeTourneau does occasional consulting and teaching for The Greeley Company, a national healthcare consulting firm, in the areas of medical staff mergers, reengineering, and physician behavior and has written articles on medical management for *Physician Executive*, ACPE's bimonthly journal, and for *Frontiers of Health Services Management*.

Wesley Curry is Managing Editor, Book Publishing, for the American College of Physician Executives. He has also served as managing editor of *Physician Executive* and of *College Digest* in his 13 years with the College. Before joining ACPE, he was managing editor of *Hospitals,* and vice president of periodicals for American Hospital Publishing, Inc., the publishing arm of the American Hospital Association.

About the Contributors

Roger M. Battistella, Ph.D., is Professor of Health Policy and Management, Sloan Graduate Program in Health Services Administration, Department of Policy Analysis and Management, Cornell University, Ithaca, New York.

Montague Brown, Dr.P.H., J.D., M.B.A., is Visiting Professor, Arizona State University, and Editor, *Health Care Management Review*.

Kenneth C. Cummings, M.D., FACPE, is Executive Vice President, Physician Integration/Services, Carondelet Health, Kansas City, Missouri.

Mark A. Doyne, M.D., FACPE, is Vice President, Medical Affairs, Curative Health Services, East Setauket, New York.

Sandra L. Gill, FACHE, FAAHC, is Founder and President of Physician Management Resources, Inc., Westmont, Illinois.

David A. Kindig, M.D., Ph.D., is Director, Wisconsin Network for Health Policy Research, University of Wisconsin Medical School, Madison, Wisconsin.

Jay Noren, M.D., M.P.H., is on the faculty in Administrative Medicine, University of Wisconsin Medical School, Madison, Wisconsin.

Joel Shalowitz, M.D., M.M., FACP, is Director/Professor, Health Services Management, Kellogg Graduate School of Management, Northwestern University, Evanston, Illinois.

Deborah Shlian, M.D., M.B.A., is President, Shlian and Associates, Boca Raton, Florida.

Thomas P. Weil, Ph.D., is President, Bedford Health Associates, Asheville, North Carolina.

Index